FRONTIER
SCHOOL TEACHERS

True Tales of the Old West

by

Charles L. Convis

Watercolor Cover by Mary Anne Convis

PIONEER PRESS, Inc., CARSON CITY, NEVADA

Library of Congress Catalog Card Number: 96-68502

ISBN 1-892156-18-0

CONTENTS

ILLUSTRATIONS

2

FIRST TEACHER IN MINNESOTA

Some teachers are remembered for the dramatic way they change students' lives. A small class in Minnesota should be remembered for the way they changed their teacher. His name was John Marsh, the first teacher in a Minnesota school.

One of the sixth generation of Marshes to live in the Salem area of Massachusetts, he expected to go to Harvard College and Harvard Medical School. Then he would take his place in the long line of a family known for producing teachers, preachers, and doctors. The oldest of seven children, the six foot, two muscular man originally wanted to be a preacher, but medical school cost less, and his immediate family were farmers.

Marsh graduated from Phillips Academy in Andover in 1819 and immediately entered Harvard. His class of 1823—about eighty students—was a strange one. By graduation time, over half had been dismissed for rebellious behavior. Marsh's dismissal had come earlier, in his sophomore year. His father, disgusted, then put him to work on the family farm.

But Marsh got a second chance on condition that he behave. Not liking farm work, he readily agreed. Harvard President John Kirkland, pleased with Marsh's scholarship and efforts to improve himself, helped. When Colonel Josiah Snelling, commanding Fort St. Anthony (present Minneapolis) asked Harvard to recommend a tutor for his sons, Kirkland chose Marsh. The colonel would provide board and lodging in his home and a salary that would let Marsh earn enough for medical school.

Marsh went to his new employment with a detachment of 5th Infantry recruits from Boston. They traveled across the Great Lakes, through the Straits of Mackinac, up the Fox and down the Wisconsin Rivers, and up the Mississippi. Since 1633, few Marshes had journeyed away from the Salem area. John Marsh was a long way from home.

About twenty officers and two hundred, fifty enlisted men, all young and full of life, garrisoned the fort. Most of the officers were West Point men and came from leading families in the East and South. But the 24-year-old graduate, fresh out of Harvard, faced a difficult group of children to teach.

Colonel Snelling had four children, Joe a son from a previous marriage, Mary, Henry, and baby James. They had only four rooms, and Marsh, used to a large, rambling farmhouse, felt cooped up rooming with the boys. The colonel, a tall, high-spirited Massachusetts man, impressed Marsh, as did his wife, Abigail. Barely older than Marsh, having married at fifteen, she had convinced the colonel to hire the tutor.

The fort had a few children other than the Snellings, and the colonel soon decided to open the school for all. The one girl besides Mary Snelling was Charlotte Ouisconsin Clark, a mixed-blood and a favorite of the regiment who had given her the unusual middle name. She and her brother Malcolm were the children of Lieutenant Nathan Clark.

Ten-year-old Mary Snelling, oldest child of the colonel and Abigail, was lovely and frail, but shy. After two years with Marsh, she went to Washington to finish her education, only to get sick and die.

Malcolm Clark, Henry Snelling, and John Tully were all about the same age, probably near ten. Full of mischief, Malcolm played the leader. He loved to ride bareback on an unbridled horse. Once, during a wolf hunt, he gripped the jaws of a captured wolf until a soldier could muzzle the animal. Quick with words and blows, Malcolm left black eyes and bloody noses in his adventurous wake.

Henry Snelling had once stirred up a hornet's nest while watching a parade for visiting General Winfield Scott. Stung in many places, Henry almost died. Another time, he fell into the river and, had it not been for a nearby soldier, would have drowned. When he recovered he told a marvelous tale of a huge catfish that had pulled him in.

Joe Snelling, the oldest at eighteen, had a drinking problem. He had entered West Point at fourteen, but was dismissed before graduation. His stepmother hated the drinking, but the colonel adored the boy.

The Tully brothers, John, nine, and Andrew, seven, had been living in the Selkirk Red River Settlement, north of present Pembina, North Dakota. Disheartened after three years of grasshoppers, bitter winters, and near starvation, the boys, their parents and baby sister were traveling south on the Red River toward Fort St. Anthony when Santee Sioux attacked.

The Indians demanded provisions from the parents who had none. The Indians struck down the parents with their war-axes, cut a hole in the ice, and threw their victims in. Then they bashed the baby's head against the ice edge and threw her in. When John saw his dying father struggle to save his wife and baby, the boy fought until overpowered by the Indians. Then, according to their custom, the Indians took the boys to their village for adoption.

After a time in the village, John took Andrew and tried to escape. They traveled at night and hid during the day. The Indians found them after three days. John fought so hard that the Indians partially scalped him.

When Colonel Snelling learned that the Indians had the boys, he sent soldiers with ransom money, and they bought the boys back. John almost died from his scalp wound. At first Andrew did not want to leave the Indian woman who had taken him in, but the soldiers finally persuaded him. This rescue had happened a few months before Marsh arrived.

Colonel Snelling took John to raise and Lieutenant Clark took Andrew. John was very depressed for the two years that Marsh taught him. Little has been written about Andrew except that he was a quiet, gentle child.

Also, little has been written about how the young teacher went about handling his strange collection of students.

Once, Marsh caught John Tully and a younger boy whispering in school. He rapped the younger boy's hand with a ruler, the standard punishment. When he attempted it with John, the boy jerked his hand away, and the ruler hit Marsh's own knee. Marsh lost his temper and he beat the boy's hand until it blistered and he was too tired to continue. Not once did John cringe or show a tear.

About a year after Marsh quit teaching, when John Tully was about twelve, the boy died of lockjaw following an axe injury. During his final illness he raved about the Indians who had killed his parents. He could be heard begging them to spare the baby and not hurt his mother. Mrs. Snelling, whom he loved dearly, had urged him to become a Christian. He regained his reason before he died, and Charlotte Clark, writing years later, said he gave clear evidence "that he loved the Savior, and felt sure that He would take him to heaven, where his father and mother and precious little sister were awaiting him."

Charlotte Clark also wrote that Marsh had a bad temper but gave him credit for making them all good readers and spellers. The curriculum had little variety. At that time reading, writing, and doing sums to the rule of three constituted a liberal education. Geography, grammar, and rhetoric were considered higher education.

Marsh enjoyed the company of the officers and enlisted men, and often played cards or drank with them in their quarters. Sometimes the parties degenerated into quarrels, followed by fights or even duels. Marsh began studying medicine while he taught school, working with Doctor Edward Purcell, the fort's surgeon.

Marsh also worked part time, carrying mail between the fort and Prairie du Chien, saving the money for medical school. The six-hundred-mile round trip through a wilderness of ice-blocked rivers, hungry wolves, and hostile Indians was dangerous. Not one civilized dwelling existed between Fort St. Anthony and Fort Crawford, a few miles from Prairie du Chien. Sometimes Marsh slept on the snow in a single blanket in temperatures of eighteen degrees below zero.

In Spring, 1825, Marsh stopped teaching and took full-time employment at Prairie du Chien as acting Indian agent. By then he had met Marguerite Decouteaux, a half-French, half-Wahpeton (Sioux) woman. The dark, beautiful, petite and graceful woman had a mind that matched Marsh's in learning languages and telling stories. Marsh had missed single women while he was teaching. He had always enjoyed talking to them, reading to them, walking with them. He liked men, but he loved being around women. Marguerite completed a perfect match, both with her beauty and her mental ability. What started as an intellectual attraction soon ripened into love. To his dying day, Marsh would say that she was the prettiest creature he had ever seen.

Marguerite's maternal grandfather had killed her French father. Then she and her mother returned to live with the Wahpetons, where Marsh met her. He described her as "the gentlest creature he ever knew, just like a fawn, clinging and affectionate." She bore him a son in February, 1826, whom they named Charles.

In 1832 Marguerite died while giving birth to a daughter, who also died. A broken-hearted Marsh had his six-year-old son baptized and then placed him with James Pantier, a doctor whom he trusted. Later that year, Marsh commanded Sioux Indians in the Blackhawk War, fighting along side the United States Army against Sauk and Fox Indians.

Then it was claimed that Marsh had illegally sold guns to the Sauk and Fox. Learning that a warrant had been issued for his arrest, he fled to St. Louis, where he joined a party of fur traders for the Rocky Mountains.

They started west on what would become the Oregon Trail but turned north to the Upper Missouri. By November Marsh was back in Independence where he opened a trader's store. Two years later he visited Dr. Pantier and Charles. The boy begged to go with his father, but Marsh said he was planning to go to California and would send for the boy.

In June, 1835, Marsh went down the Santa Fe Trail, was captured by Comanches, escaped, and eventually reached the small pueblo of Los Angeles in February, 1836. He obtained a license to practice medicine, the first doctor in California. His practice among Mexicans, Californians, and Yankees grew, but he closed his office in September and rode north, looking for a place to raise cattle.

He found it in the north end of the San Joaquin Valley. He bought a 50,000 acre ranch extending from Mount Diablo, overlooking San Francisco Bay, to the San Joaquin River, forty miles east. He resumed medical practice, taking his pay in cattle to stock the ranch. He charged high fees, fifty cattle for delivering a baby, three hundred for a trip to San Jose.

Marsh wrote to Charles, but the letter had to go around Cape Horn to Boston and then west to the frontier. Charles never got it. When Marsh never got an answer, he assumed the boy was dead.

In June, 1851, Marsh married Abigail Tuck, a school teacher in Santa Clara. She was from Massachusetts, tall and good looking. She had come to California a year before with Baptist missionaries. She had turned down many marriage proposals. Marsh did not tell her about Marguerite and

Charles. Neither had he ever told his parents and family about them.

Abby and Marsh had a daughter, Alice, in March, 1852, and Abby died in 1855.

In March, 1856, a seedy, hungry-looking man of about thirty knocked on Marsh's door, begging for a place to spend the night. When Marsh realized that it was his son, he broke down and cried.

Charles told his father that he had married a niece of James Pantier, and they had three children. With no news, Charles had assumed his father was dead until a returned argonaut mentioned that he had seen a man in California who looked exactly like Charles.

"My father was a doctor," Charles had said.

"And this man is a doctor, too. You have the same eyes, the same nose, the same carriage."

Charles's wife did not want him to go on a wild goose chase, so he slipped away without telling her. He went down the Mississippi, across the gulf of Mexico and the Isthmus, and took a steamer to San Francisco. He walked the last twenty-five miles. A joyous Marsh assured Charles that he would send for the rest of the boy's family so they could share his beautiful home and huge ranch with him and his little daughter.

Marsh had been paying his *vaqueros* twenty-five cents for each calf they branded. After the 1855 branding had been completed, they demanded a dollar for each calf. Marsh took them to court and won, but they hated him, and their resentment grew.

A few months after his reunion with Charles and while he looked forward to meeting his daughter-in-law and grandchildren and sharing his home with them, Marsh had to go to San Francisco on business. On September 24, 1856, he was riding his buggy near Martinez when three of his *vaqueros* attacked him.

Marsh fought valiantly and he knocked one of the assailants to the ground and throttled him, but three young men with knives were too much for the fifty-seven-year-old man. With blood pouring from his mouth and his side, and many knife wounds in his body, he finally slumped into the dust, dead.

His magnificent stone house, probably the finest in California, and the large ranch were divided between his two children. California's first doctor never went to Harvard Medical School as he wanted. How much his class affected the first teacher in Minnesota is a mystery, but he sure broke from the mold of six generations of Massachusetts Marshes.

Suggested reading: George D. Lyman, *John Marsh, Pioneer* (New York: Charles Scribner's Sons, 1930).

ISOLATION IN LITTLE RUSSIA

L inda Slaughter was twenty-eight when she came to Dakota Territory in 1871 with her husband, the post surgeon at Fort Randall. She became Dakota's first composer, creating three songs about military life.

By 1875, she had been appointed Bismarck's first postmistress. Linda was also a fine writer. Her description of a two-month teaching position in February and March, 1887, in an Emmons County rural school is revealing about conditions in North Dakota's early schools.

To reach her school, Linda traveled from Bismarck thirty miles south by stage to Emmonsburg at the mouth of Beaver Creek on the east side of the Missouri River. The weekly stage up the creek had already gone, so Postmaster Harmidas Archambault took her in his wagon to Dakem, fourteen miles east of present Linton, where she was to teach. The Archambault family impressed Linda. The Frenchman had an Indian wife, and their two daughters, both convent educated, were accomplished young ladies.

Archambault and Linda stopped at the Omio post office for dinner. She described the postmistress as a sorrowful woman whose husband had deserted her. The summer before, her crippled son had died, her daughter had drowned in the creek that flowed past her door, and the daughter's son had committed suicide. In addition, her seventeen-year-old son was in the Bismarck penitentiary for murdering a Russian who had stolen his pony.

Linda and her driver approached Dakem through deep snow. They met the school clerk on his way to a housewarming and dance. With no place else to stay in Dakem, they turned around and followed the clerk to the dance. Dakem was a community of Germans from Russia.

The people at the dance included the sorrowful postmistress from Omio, and a family of Bohemians (Czechs) who lived ten miles away. After a hot supper at midnight, Linda fell asleep. She woke at daybreak, the dancing still lively.

Linda rode back to Dakem with the school clerk in a straw-filled open sleigh. The school clerk's family were the only English speaking people in the settlement. Their two story house impressed Linda.

Apparently most of the people dressed in Russian fashion, with home made cowhide shoes and pointed hats. Linda commented on the sheepskin coat worn by the president of the school board. She said he wore the wool inside with the leather out, opposite to the way of the sheep. [Buffalo coats were made with the fur out, but this writer is unaware if sheepskin coats were ever made that way.]

A yoke of oxen pulled Linda on a sleigh five miles to the home where she would board. As the clerk's house disappeared in the distance, she felt

8

like a shipwrecked sailor who sees a friendly sail vanishing on the horizon. Her companions chattered in Russian, occasionally giving her a friendly nod that everything was fine.

Their house, buried to the eaves in snow, had sod walls, plastered on the outside with a mortar of cow dung and pebbles. A cow stood in one of the two doors. They passed through the other door to the family quarters. The first room, filled to the ceiling with straw and cow dung to be burned in the stove, led to a small, dark kitchen with one tiny window. The kitchen had a stone stove, six feet high, plastered with ashes and sand.

The kitchen led to the "best" room, where the rest of the family rose to greet their guest. Besides the grown son and son-in-law who drove the oxen, the family was the "old couple" parents and the married daughter with her two small children, a boy and a girl. The heavy, broad-shouldered women wore full Russian skirts with loose blouses, heavy shoes, and red kerchiefs on their heads. The men wore sheepskin garments.

The room had a board floor and whitewashed walls, covered with pictures of saints, a crucifix, and rosaries. Large willow baskets containing extra clothing hung from ceiling hooks. Two large bedsteads were piled high with feather beds. Light came from two small, double-paned windows, set deep into the sod walls.

At supper time the whole family moved to a special corner of the room to cross themselves and pray. Supper was boiled potatoes, boiled pork, and boiled sauerkraut, served in earthen crocks. They made a new bed for Linda from lumber and placed two featherbeds on it.

After their breakfast of fried potatoes, fried pork, and fried sauerkraut, they took Linda to her school two miles away on a horse-drawn sled made from two logs covered with short boards. Linda's seat was a sack filled with hay which the horse would eat at noon. The driver sat in front of her and the children in back. Linda had trouble keeping her balance as the sled lurched over the drifted snow. Finally the driver shifted the long scarf he wore for a belt until its loops were at his back, and he indicated for Linda to hang on to those. The children laughed, and she felt embarrassed, but she clung to the loops as one would a life preserver.

As they neared their destination, similar sleds approached from all directions. Many were drawn by an ox. One was drawn by a cow, who contributed her milk to the children's lunch.

The farmhouse used as a school was a low sod building, almost buried by snowdrifts. A friendly woman in Russian dress met Linda at the door and showed her the schoolroom, which was the family's living room. The adjoining room contained bins of wheat and flaxseed, and a calf.

The schoolroom had an earthen floor with whitewashed walls. A long table with benches on each side took up one wall, and two featherbeds took up the opposite wall. A baby, whose dress was a miniature copy of her mother's, even to the red head scarf, lay on one of the beds. The students ranged in age from five to twenty. They sat on the benches or stood with their backs to the wall. A few knew a little English, but the majority did not know the alphabet. They were all fairly well advanced in arithmetic.

The head of the family and a member of the school board came in, sat on stools, smoked cigarettes, and listened to the recitations with rapt attention. At noon the books were set aside, and the family, teacher, and guests ate a dinner of boiled potatoes, boiled pork, and boiled sauerkraut. Apparently the school children brought their own dinners. After dinner, the woman of the house cleaned the stable part of the building while her husband shoveled snow off the roof and cut paths to the straw stacks.

Another sled arrived in the afternoon bringing four small boys and their father. The man could speak a little English and he proudly introduced his sons, eleven, ten, nine, and eight.

"A nice family," Linda said.

"Oh, got plenty more at home smaller as these."

"Are you Russian?"

He indignantly replied that he was German, not Russian. His people had lived in Odessa, Russia, since their ancestors immigrated from Germany a hundred years before. Russian law required them to speak Russian, send their children to Russian schools, and conform to the country's customs. But at home, the children spoke German and learned to love the Fatherland.

The ride home was not so comfortable, as the horse had eaten the bag of hay. Linda got better at riding the sled, even handling the almost-daily upset with equanimity. She grew to like her students and to respect their parents who were so eager to have them learn American ways. She even looked forward to the daily meals of potatoes, pork, and sauerkraut, sometimes boiled, sometimes fried.

Linda Slaughter had a post office named for her. Established in Solitude, a settlement near Willow in Burleigh County, the name was changed to Slaughter, and the population reached twenty-six by the 1890s. Then it declined and the post office closed in 1908.

Except for the feeling that she had been exiled from her native country, Linda always had fond memories of her short teaching assignment.

Suggested reading: Warren Henke and Everett Albers, Eds. *The Legacy of North Dakota's Country Schools* (Bismarck: North Dakota Humanities Council, 1998).

LOVE AT EARLY SIGHT

Anna Maria Pittman, oldest of thirteen children in the family of a wealthy New York City manufacturer, received a fine education. A gifted poet and deeply religious, her life goal was to become a missionary school teacher and convert Indians to Christianity. She got her chance in 1836 when she was thirty-three years old.

The year before, Methodist preacher Jason Lee had established the Willamette Mission in Oregon. He asked the Methodist Mission Board to send two single women out to teach. The board selected Anna Maria and Elvira Johnson. On July 29, 1836, they sailed from Boston, along with a blacksmith and his family, a doctor and his family, and the fiancee of another preacher, already at the mission.

Her companions on the journey hinted that Anna Maria had been selected to be Jason Lee's wife.

"I'm interested only in Christianity and teaching," she insisted. "If that should change, I'll decide for myself who to marry."

After twenty two thousand miles by way of Hawaii and the passage of ten months, the reinforcements reached Fort Vancouver, a Hudson's Bay post on the Columbia River. Jason Lee met them and led them to his mission.

Apparently the mission board had suggested to Lee that they had sent Anna Maria to be his wife. He kept an open mind, but replied to curious associates that he would never marry unless satisfied *on acquaintance* that such a step would be conducive to their mutual happiness and to the glory of God.

In fact, Lee had once been introduced to Anna Maria in New York, and he was not impressed. He had written in his diary then that she was a lady of deep piety and good sense, but he would "never fancy her as a wife." After the meeting at Fort Vancouver, he wrote in his diary that he still had the same prejudice toward her.

The initial attitudes about matrimony began changing during the two-day canoe trip to the mission. Anna Maria was assigned to Jason's canoe. On June 5, 1837, nine days after their arrival, she wrote her parents:

"You will be anxious to know if there is any prospect of my having a Protector. Let me tell you there is. Mr. J. Lee has broached the subject. It remains for me to say whether I shall be his helpmate in this important charge. I look upon the Lord who has thus far directed me in the path of duty to enable me prayerfully to investigate the subject. . . . I expect to give my heart and hand to J. Lee. When this union shall take place I am not prepared to say."

Anna Maria taught Sundays at the mission school with its thirty children. During the week she cooked their food and made their clothing. She started out making twelve pounds of butter each week, but the mission added eighty cows to their herd, and the weekly churning increased.

The mission reinforcements, all familiar with the Methodist hymnal, added their singing talents to the worship services. Trappers and traders started bringing their Indian wives. Mission activities increased, and so did the courting between Anna Maria and Jason. They found time for long horseback rides and canoe trips together, as they delivered important messages to neighbors and carried out mission business.

He proposed four weeks after her arrival. She gave her answer in poetry, based on the Book of Ruth:

> "Yes, where thou goest I will go,
>   With thine my earthly lot be cast;
> In pain or pleasure, joy or woe,
>   Will I attend thee to the last.
>
> "That hour shall find me by thy side,
>   And where thy grave is, mine shall be;
> Death can but for a time divide,
>   My firm and faithful heart from thee.
>
> "Thy people and thy charge be mine,
>   Thy God, my God shall ever be;
> All that I have receive as thine,
>   My heart and hand I give to thee.
>
> "And as through life we glide along,
>   Through tribulation's troubled sea:
> Still let our faith in God be strong,
>   And confidence unshaken be."

Plans had long been made to have Oregon's first public communion service on Sunday, July 16, 1837. The missionaries had encouraged trappers and traders to marry the Indian women they claimed as wives. To set an example, Cyrus Shepard, preacher who helped Lee establish the mission, and Susan Downing, his fiancee who traveled west with Anna Maria and Elvira Johnson, decided to get married that day. Anna Maria and Jason also decided to marry that day, but kept it secret from all but Jason's nephew, Daniel, who was to perform the ceremony.

The congregation assembled for a beautiful outdoor service among gigantic fir trees. After the opening hymn and prayers, Jason preached a short sermon about the importance of marriage as an institution.

"Example speaks louder than precept," he said. "I have long been convinced that if we would have others practice what we recommend, circumstances being equal, we must set them the example."

Then to the surprise of all but Anna Maria and his nephew, he stepped down from his outdoor pulpit, took Anna Maria by the hand, and led her to the altar. Daniel stepped up to the pulpit and conducted the ceremony.

Jason returned Anna Maria to her seat, and replaced his nephew in the pulpit to marry Cyrus Shepard and Susan Downing, who may have been wondering if they had just been pre-empted.

The day turned out to be a triple wedding. We don't know if the third was planned or if the couple got caught up in the excitement, but Charles Roe brought Nancy, a Callapooya Indian girl, forward to finish a momentous occasion.

After another sermon by Jason Lee, Charles Roe was baptized and received into the church. No mention was made of Nancy's baptism. Hopefully, she was omitted only in the account, not in the occasion.

A great wedding day for a pious woman! Anna Maria was the first white woman married in Oregon. On that wonderful day, fourteen took communion, many testified to the goodness of God, and two were baptized and admitted into the church.

Anna Maria's happiness did not last long. The mission decided that Jason should ride east and advise the board in person about their needs in Oregon. Jason rode away, with companions, on March 26, 1838. They had been married eight months, and Anna Maria was soon to become a mother.

The boy, born June 23, lived two days. His mother died the next day. The beautiful grove where Anna Maria had exchanged marriage vows less than a year before now had a grave containing the bodies of the first white child born in Oregon and the first white woman to die there.

The news that he had lost his wife and son caught up with Jason Lee at the Shawnee Mission, near Westport, Missouri, on September 8.

Elvira Johnson Perkins, Anna Maria's traveling companion, sent the Pittmans the first news of their daughter's death. Elvira had been moved to another post on the Columbia River, and she got the tragic news on July 5. She wrote the parents that she never saw their daughter "in so happy a state of mind as for a season before I was called to leave her for this station. She seemed perfectly resigned to the will of God, and ripening for heaven."

Jason Lee married Lucy Thompson of Vermont on July 28, 1839, ten months after learning of his wife's death. We don't know how Anna

Maria's parents learned this, but her mother attacked Jason on two grounds: first, for re-marrying before he had even seen Anna Maria's grave; second, for not telling them in advance.

Jason and his new bride sailed for Oregon in November. He wrote to Mrs. Pittman on November 27. He claimed that countless persons had urged him to remarry, begging him to not return to Oregon alone. He mentioned a visit to the Pittmans, which may have been when Mrs. Pittman expressed her outrage about his quick remarriage.

He wrote: "I must add, that the impression of our reception at your house, remains indelibly fixed upon my mind, and holds a prominent place, among the few incidents of my life, to which I cannot revert without extreme pain."

As if that insult to a grieving mother were not enough, he gave as the reason for not telling her of his re-marriage plans that she was hard of hearing! He was afraid that speaking loud enough for her to hear would enable eavesdroppers to learn his plans.

Besides his new wife, Jason Lee took with him to Oregon the grave marker for the first one. The long inscription refers to Anna Maria Pittman, wife of Rev. Jason Lee. Mrs. Pittman may have wondered why it didn't refer to the *first* wife of Jason Lee, since he had decided to remarry by the time he ordered the marker.

In a December 11, 1839, letter from Rio de Janeiro (perhaps the last to his first in-laws) Jason Lee wrote:

"May our Common Father and gracious benefactor crown the evening of your days with his loving kindness and tender mercies and bring you safely to his eternal joy. Give my love to all the family, and tell them that I am a witness to some of the many strong cries that their dear departed sister offered up for them, while she was here in the flesh. Her voice is hushed in death! And I now beseech you, in her stead, yea, in Christ's stead, to be reconciled to God, that they may meet their dear sister in heaven."

We might understand if Mrs. Pittman wondered why their family needed a reminder about being reconciled to God.

Suggested reading: Theressa Gay, *Life and Letters of Mrs. Jason Lee* (Portland: Metropolitan Press, 1936).

FRUSTRATION IN OREGON

Margaret Jewett Smith was a member of the second reinforcement sent out to the Methodist Mission in the Willamette Valley of Oregon. She traveled around Cape Horn with a small group led by Reverend David Leslie, reaching Oregon in fall 1837.

In a day when young ladies were expected to be silent and submissive, Margaret was neither. She had been raised on a Massachusetts farm, and her father considered higher education for women an abomination to the Lord. She went to the Wilbraham Academy anyway, and prepared for a teaching career.

On the journey west, Margaret nursed Reverend Leslie's chronically ill wife and cared for his three daughters. Nevertheless, he treated her as a social inferior and harassed her constantly. When they reached Oregon, they weren't speaking to each other.

Margaret filed formal charges against Reverend Leslie, saying he had oppressed her. She also demanded formal recognition of her status as a teacher. Reverend Jason Lee, head of the mission, told her bluntly he would not entertain the charges and he didn't need another teacher.

Margaret found a teaching position at Fort Vancouver. A month later, the mission relented and allowed her back to teach. But her relation to the mission remained volatile. Once she invited some Indians inside where Leslie was preaching. Shortly after they entered the small, poorly-ventilated room, the Indians were asked to go outside to the porch where they could listen to the gospel while sitting in the breeze. The Indians left and so did Margaret.

Margaret organized the Oregon Female Benevolent Society to teach Indian women how to sew. When the mission refused to give the women scraps of cloth, she wrote to friends in the East, asking for contributions. She pointed out that the mission was already selling goods and clothing that had been donated by eastern contributors.

One of the mission staff, carpenter William Willson, set out after Margaret with matrimony in mind. He seemed anxious to marry someone. He had just sent a letter back to Connecticut, asking a woman named Chloe Clark to come out and be his wife. Margaret, spurned by others at the mission, responded to Willson. But she demanded written proof that his other engagement was canceled before she would marry.

The mission decided that winter that Margaret and Willson would have to share a tiny cabin. As the nights got longer and colder, the muslin barrier between their beds became less of a barrier to Willson. But Margaret held firm in her resolve.

"We're already livin' together jist like man and wife," Willson insisted. "All 'cept the most important part, anyways."

"Nothing doing, until I see it in writing."

With mail delivery measured by seasons, Willson had a cold winter. Finally, after a particularly intense discussion, he ran from the cabin, saying he would destroy her reputation.

Willson told Reverend Leslie that he and Margaret had sinned grievously. Some of the mission staff reveled in joyous indignation, as Willson repeated his confession to all. His loud lamentations were matched by his tearful repentance.

Leslie waited in vain for Margaret's admission of carnal sin. He even tried stealth. He told her of two preachers who had committed such sins. After they confessed and married, all was forgiven.

"I've done nothing wrong," Margaret said. "There's nothing to confess."

But Willson hoped to become a minister himself, and he worked hard toward that goal. The mission didn't want him subject to the accusation that he, himself, was a false accuser. So they prepared a written confession and presented it to Margaret. They told her she would have to acknowledge her sin; the brethren would accept nothing else. She felt trapped. She depended on the mission for food and shelter, and had no other prospects. She signed.

Shortly after her confession, Margaret married William J. Bailey, an English doctor who made up in education and ability what he lacked in physical appearance. A few years before, Bailey had been attacked by a Rogue River Indian. The Indian struck Bailey's head with an axe, cleaving his mouth and both jaws. The axe drove deeply into his neck, barely missing the carotid artery. Somehow he had managed to travel three hundred miles to the mission, holding his shattered face together as best he could. The wound healed into a grotesque mass of lumpy flesh and mangled bones, beyond the power of surgical repair.

Bailey became one of the main founders of the government of Oregon. But he was also a heavy drinker. Margaret divorced him in 1852. Three years later, she married again and also divorced that husband.

Margaret Smith Bailey (????) was an Oregon teacher who found neither professional satisfaction, acceptance, love, nor fortune. She died in poverty in 1882.

Suggested reading: Malcom Clark, Jr., *Eden Seekers* (Boston: Houghton Mifflin Company, 1981).

A WOMAN OF GRIT

The first English-speaking school in California opened in Santa Clara in December, 1846. The teacher, Olive Isbell, was a woman of determination and grit.

Olive and her husband, Dr. Isaac Isbel, left Greenbush, Illinois, in April, 1846, to travel by covered wagon to California. Well-outfitted and carrying two thousand dollars in savings, they escaped some of the hardships faced by other travelers.

News of the declaration of war against Mexico reached their 23-wagon train while it rested at Fort Hall. Riders galloped into the fort from the west shouting that anyone going to California, then part of Mexico, would be killed. Dr. Isbell asked his young wife if they should turn back. Her firm reply came quickly.

"I started for California, and I want to go on," she said.

Her determination inspired others, and the majority of the train traveled on. They crossed the Sierras without dismantling their wagons, only the second train to accomplish that feat. No one in the train was certain about the way to California, so when they reached a ranch in October, they asked which way to go.

"You're in California now," they were told. "This is the Johnson Ranch on the Bear River. Most of the emigrants come through here. They're usually ready for a rest after crossing the mountains."

The Isbell train knew nothing of the difficulties experienced by another train from Illinois — the Donner-Reed train. A few weeks behind, it experienced a snowbound winter of starvation and death.

Olive's train rested for a week's at Sutter's Fort. Then soldiers of John C. Fremont escorted it to the Mission Santa Clara de Asis. The soldiers barricaded the immigrants inside the mission for an expected winter of war against the Californios.

Fremont drafted Dr. Isbell for service with his battalion, and the young bride, left behind with the women, children and disabled, again had her courage tested. Her husband came down with emigrant fever (typhoid pneumonia) and returned to the mission. Olive nursed him back to health, as she had others who were sick. She handed out over a hundred doses of medicine each day, and then carried ammunition to the sentries at night.

Fremont's battalion marched south, and the people barricaded inside the mission discovered kegs of gunpowder, apparently concealed by Californios. Fearing an attempt to blow up the mission, they sent a messenger to the American troops at San Jose. Twenty-five Marines from

Yerba Buena (present San Francisco) commanded by Captain Ward Marston came to the rescue.

As the marines approached the mission on January 2, 1847, their cannon bogged down in the mud while a force of one hundred twenty Californios under Francisco Sánchez attacked. After four Californios were killed and five wounded, with two Marines wounded among the defenders, Olive's handkerchief served as a flag of truce to stop the firing. Five days later a treaty ended the only battle in northern California during the War Against Mexico.

With the war over and her husband well, Olive thought about the two dozen children, some of them orphans, at the mission. She had been a teacher before her marriage, and she decided to set up a school. With the children's help, she turned a horse stable, measuring sixteen feet square, into a classroom. Their random collection of books included a few McGuffey's Readers, some spellers, and one or two arithmetic and geography books. They had no blackboard. Olive wrote her lesson assignments on the dirt floor with a pointed stick.

After two months of school, Olive and her husband and five other families moved to Monterey. The fame of her little mission school had spread, and she was asked to start another. This time, a room in the Monterey Custom House became a classroom, and Olive started with twenty-six pupils. Attendance soon swelled to fifty-six. Olive got help from some of the boys who spoke English, as she could not speak Spanish.

So this intrepid woman, a young bride from the East in a foreign land with a heart filled with grit, not only started the first English-speaking school in California, but she also started the second!

Suggested reading: Thelma M. Wible, "Olive M. Isbell, Teacher, Nurse, Hero," in *True West, v. 29, No. 11* (November, 1982).

CIVICS LESSON

Montana probably had the best excuse for vigilante justice in the Old West. Not only was there no law during the early gold rush, but the mastermind behind a wave of robberies and killings that totaled over a hundred murders was the sheriff himself. Henry Plummer got elected sheriff of both Bannack and Virginia City so he would know which stages carried gold and could cover for his gang of road agents and killers.

When the Committee of Vigilance secretly organized in December, 1863, it wasted no time in attacking frontier anarchy. No one knows who they all were, but the most responsible citizens—a future governor, men who would become senators, marshals, and prosecuting attorneys, leading citizens of all kinds, even a future president of the United States—at least supported them if they did not actively participate.

During the Christmas recess the children in the Bannack school knew that ominous events were unfolding. Small groups of miners collecting along Grasshopper Creek to break up as strangers approached, and hushed voices of their parents in the evenings told them something was afoot.

Then came that trial in nearby Nevada City on December 21. Wilbur Sanders, their teacher's cousin and a lawyer, had not been here long enough to be afraid, and they chose him to prosecute George Ives for murder before a jury of hundreds of miners. When the miners shouted their guilty verdict, Ives asked for a little time to write his mother and sisters in Wisconsin. Then a man with a strange name, X Biedler, spoke up: "Sanders, ask him how much time he gave the Dutchman."

The people were certainly fed up with lawlessness.

Before Ives was hanged he talked about others in the gang, including their secret boss, and the children wondered what might happen.

Sidney Edgerton, appointed by President Lincoln to head the Territorial Supreme Court, had donated the room for their school, and his niece, Lucia Darling, became their teacher. With improvised desks and books collected from the community, they started school in October. Less than three months ago! Now that Edgerton's nephew—the teacher's cousin—had prosecuted Ives, and Ives had sung like a mine canary before he danced on the air, would something happen to the school? Then two more were hanged on New Years day, and the children continued to worry.

On Sunday, January 10, 1864, Lucia sat in the schoolroom and worried, too. Just four months ago, their party of seventeen from Tallmadge, Ohio, most of them related, had reached Bannack, where Montana gold was first discovered. The place was crowded, and all Uncle Sidney could find for a home was an abandoned store building that had been

LUCIA DARLING

Montana Historical Society

partitioned into five rooms. When some parents learned that Lucia had been a grade school teacher back in Ohio, they wanted to start a school. She agreed to become Montana's first teacher, but they were unable to find a room until Edgerton gave up one of his.

Now Lucia sat at the window in that room, looking up the gulch and the snowy hillside where the gallows that Sheriff Plummer had built and used stood out against the sky in all its naked ugliness. Would the children come tomorrow or was school all over after a short three months? And could the ugly things being whispered about the sheriff be true? Just a few weeks ago, she and cousin Wilbur, who had been discharged from honorable Civil War military service, and Uncle Sidney, the president's choice for the supreme court, had been his guests at Thanksgiving.

Henry Plummer was a strange man. In his late twenties, five feet ten, slender, and good-looking, he had bowed gallantly for Lucia. He talked intelligently about the war, about books, about the future of the territory in which they would all prosper together. He looked like a gentleman, but his eyes were flat, cold, gray, and expressionless. He seemed to look right through you, but a quick, mouth-only smile made one forget about the glassy stare. Leading citizens sought his opinions and welcomed him into their homes. He could flatter ladies with perfect propriety, but he was equally at home in saloons.

People wondered why he kept a fine saddle-horse at a ranch near Bannack but never brought it into town. Where did he go on those prospecting trips that always seemed to coincide with a holdup? Could the ugly rumors that he was the leader behind all those unsolved crimes be true?

Then Lucia heard crowd noise and she looked again through the icy window and saw a small group traveling up the gulch. Three of them had their hands tied. The others had masks or hoods concealing their identity. Two men carried a small table and others had ropes.

They stopped at the gallows and set the table up under the crossbar. Lucia rubbed a wider viewing area on the cold window. Watching the men horrified her, but she couldn't stop. She thought of her twenty students, aged six to sixteen. Some had been in school before, but for most it was their first experience. How many might be watching? How many had fathers or uncles in the crowd that was now following up the gulch? She only taught reading, writing, sums, and geography. What if she had to teach civics, what could she say? And where was the sheriff? Why didn't he prevent this illegal dispensation of justice without trial?

The masked men threw ropes over the top rail of the gallows and seemed to be fitting a loop over the head of one of the three men whom they had lifted up to the table. Another seemed to be protesting violently. Lucia wanted to close her eyes, but couldn't. She kept wondering if some of her students would have questions tomorrow that she should have answers for. But where could she find the answers?

Then two masked men jerked the table away, and the man in the rope dropped, his head bent to one side, his neck broken. They did the same to the second man, and the third one seemed to be begging now for his life. When all three twisted slowly in the air their feet kicking wildly, Lucia felt sick to her stomach. As the twitching stopped and the bodies swayed in the icy wind, the crowd, following up the gulch, pointed and waved their arms in joy. Lucia turned away, rubbing tears from her cheeks.

She sat alone for a time, still wondering if she would have answers for impossible questions tomorrow. Then she heard the shouting in the street. She went to the door and learned that the three bodies at the top of the gulch were the sheriff and two of his deputies. It was the sheriff who had begged for his life.

No one asked questions the next day and Lucia was glad. They heard a loud explosion in the afternoon and she sent the children home for the day. That evening she learned that the only Mexican in Bannack had his cabin shelled with a howitzer and set on fire. Then he was riddled with bullets and left to burn. Later two of Bannack's prostitutes probed through the ashes, looking for gold, either from the Mexican's reputed hoard or from his teeth.

On Wednesday that week of death, five men were hanged at one time in nearby Virginia City.

Lucia went to her uncle and said she was going back to Ohio. She could no longer live in such a heathenish place. He talked to her long and patiently. He pointed out what she had already accomplished in the community, and how much the children needed her help and influence. Finally, with some misgivings, she agreed to stay.

Sidney Edgerton became Montana's first territorial governor. Wilbur Sanders was the state's first United States Senator. John X. Biedler became the territorial marshal. Granville Stuart, the father of Montana, very likely had an important role with the vigilantes. We know that rancher Theodore Roosevelt supported them.

Lucia Darling certainly wondered what effect the untaught lessons about government had on her first students in Montana. The short reign of vigilantes probably had some excesses—the killing of Frank Pizanthia on the day school resumed appeared to be one—but it is hard to imagine what Montana would have become but for the short vigilante rule.

Lucia came to feel pride that she had been Montana's first teacher.

Suggested reading: Beatrice J. Johnson, "Hazards of the Pioneer School Teacher" in *The West, v.* 8, No. 3 (February, 1968).

DIFFICULTIES AT FORT DES MOINES

For six years after 1848 the National Popular Education Board sponsored almost six hundred single women from northern New England and upper New York state to travel west and teach. Catherine Beecher, founder of the Board, was older sister to Henry Ward Beecher, America's most prominent preacher, and to Harriet Beecher Stowe, leading humanitarian and writer. Catherine had already established a small, private school in Hartford, Connecticut. She wanted the Board to send only Evangelical Protestants out to teach. When others did not share her zeal to compete with Catholics, she left the Board. But only graduates from Protestant female seminaries were sent.

Only a few crossed the Mississippi River. They included twenty-four-year-old Arozina Perkins from Vermont, assigned to Fort Des Moines, Iowa. Arozina dedicated her life to education, truth, and religion. Her grandfather had been a Baptist minister. She had a mentally ill sister and a brother in jail. She dreamed grandly about sharing in the redemption of the West, where two million children had no teachers.

Arozina's 1850 journey west took forty-one days. She traveled by train to Buffalo, boat to Cleveland, train to Cincinnati, boat to Keokuk, Iowa, and mud wagon and stage to Fort Des Moines, arriving on November 13.

She had a poor reception. The town had one church and one school. The teacher was the preacher's wife. She had forty pupils and didn't need help. Apparently the only person who knew she was coming was the lawyer who requested the Board to send her. The community knew nothing of the Board and questioned Arozina's motives. "They seem to regard me as an adventurer," she wrote.

She did get a school with nine pupils. Within a month, she was up to twenty-four.

Arozina had been writing to a young minister whom she hoped to marry. She finally told him in January about the brother in jail. She was not surprised when he wrote to break off their relationship, saying the jail sentence might hurt his career. However, Arozina was bitterly disappointed. She wrote in her diary:

"He has discarded me because I am so unfortunate as to have a prodigal brother. Perhaps it is well, for this fact might have been a barrier to his usefulness in the ministry. But if he, who professed to love me so well, has turned from me, what am I to expect from those who feel no interest in me? Will not all the good and high minded despise me?" She never married.

Her first school term ended on February 7, 1851. She doubted that she had collected enough tuition to pay her expenses. She spent her last dime on postage for a letter to her brother in jail.

Four days later Arozina visited the local jail, as part of her church mission work. She talked to a young man awaiting trial for murder. His sister was there and seemed very dejected. "Oh how I pitied her," a sympathetic Arizona wrote.

The next day, she learned that her own brother was free again. We have no indication that she ever told that to the minister whom she had hoped to marry.

In her second term she had thirty-two pupils. The youngest was five, the oldest a single woman about forty. She also had three young men and a married woman. Arozina was twenty-five.

Arozina loved to fish. She and friends styled themselves the "Hook and Line Company of Fort Des Moines, and they fished often. It was probably the only part of life in that frontier town that did not disappoint her. As she neared the end of her second term, she received an offer to teach at the Fairfield, Iowa, Female Seminary. She sought advice from the lawyer who had asked that she be sent out and apparently forgot to tell anyone. She was disappointed that he was so sparing in advice. She wrote: "Perhaps it is because he is a lawyer, and has been accustomed to be paid for it."

As she agonized with her decision, Arozina wrote:

"'Tis a difficult matter for me to decide about leaving here. When I look upon all this region as missionary ground, and consider the yet unformed state of society, and all the old and absurd notions entertained by some of the people who have been all their lives Westerners, I feel it is my duty to remain and throw in my mite towards the molding of the mass into a pleasant and perfect form. I am becoming acquainted with and like the people. I have weathered difficulties and even sufferings which I never before experienced, and to abandon the field now would seem unwise, and, perhaps, wrong. Though I have received no compensation in a worldly shape, I have the satisfaction of knowing that I have been striving for a higher reward than earth can give."

Her Fairfield salary would be three times as much as she could expect to make in Fort Des Moines. The seminary was a boarding school for young ladies. She decided to take the job. They assigned her to their advanced scholars.

Suggested reading: Polly W. Kaufman, *Women Teachers on the Frontier* (New Haven: Yale University Press, 1984).

THE PROFESSOR

The first school in the Colorado gold fields was established in Auraria (now part of Denver) in 1859. In August that year O. J. Goldrick came thundering down Cherry Creek with a wagon and team of oxen. With his silk hat, immaculate linen shirt, and broadcloth frock coat, in the pockets of which he had a B.A. from the University of Dublin, and an M.A. from Columbia University, he did not look like a bullwhacker.

Goldrick coiled his whip and brought his rambunctious oxen to a halt in front of Dick Wooton's saloon. With a striped trouser leg braced against the brake, his yellow, doeskin-gloved hands calmly holding the bull whip, and the Denver dust settling around his wagon, he gracefully doffed his hat at the gathering onlookers. Earlier, he had stopped a mile outside the settlement to adorn his silk waistcoat with lilies of the valley, rosebuds, and violets in a blooming burst of native beauty.

"What brings yuh here to Cherry Creek?" a bystander asked.

In a voice heavy with Irish brogue, the clean-shaven teamster from County Sligo replied, "*Majura verum iritia!*"

"What the hell kinda Injun lingo is that?" his questioner asked.

"That, my dear fellow is Latin." Goldrick bowed his head and smiled. "And it means the beginning of greater things."

"You must be a professor," hotelman David Smoke observed.

With that entrance, Goldrick's place in Colorado's history was assured.

"What wuz yuh yellin at them bulls?" another onlooker asked. "It don't sound like nuthin we ever heerd before."

"Merely classical objurations on which they relish, my good man."

"Is you a school teacher? We need one of them. Something to keep these young sprouts oughta ourn hair when we's digging fer gold."

Goldrick had one coin to his name, a fifty-cent piece. He recognized an opportunity. "I might consider it. What's the salary?"

"Jist pass the hat and ye'll find out. We kin find a place fer ye to set up yer shop."

The amused and impressed onlookers began digging into their pockets. Goldrick's dark, silk hat soon held two hundred fifty dollars. He started teaching in a one-room log cabin on Blake Street.

An open hole in the gable provided the only light, and the opening for a door was covered by canvas from a wagon top. Thirteen scholars made up his first class — "two Indians, two Mexicans, and the rest white, but from Missouri," he described them in a letter to John D. Philbrick, superintendent of schools at Boston.

A few weeks after the school opened, Lewis Tappan from Massachusetts walked past one Sunday and saw children playing in front. When he asked why they were in the street, they explained that school was in recess.

Tappan stuck his head in the door. "Goldrick, do you mean to tell me that you teach this school seven days a week?"

"Of course. Their parents are delighted. It keeps them out from under foot."

Settlers, proud of their first school, met wagons with the cry, "Now we've got a school." They urged immigrants with children to settle down there. Enrollments increased rapidly. Two more private schools started in Denver within a year, and schools opened in Central City, Blackhawk, Georgetown, and Boulder.

Not content with starting the first school, Goldrick also started the first Denver library in 1860 with one book from his personal collection. He called it the Denver and Auraria Reading Room Association. He also promoted the settlement's first Sunday School.

Goldrick began contributing articles to the *Rocky Mountain News.* The owners made him an editor. In 1864, when a sudden flood roared down Cherry Creek, sweeping away bridges, homes, the city jail, the building housing the *News* and its 3000 pound printing press, and drowning hundreds of cattle and about twenty people, Goldrick wrote up the disaster. His long lead sentence reveals the baroque schoolmaster style which his scholars had to endure every day. He wrote:

"About the midnight hour of Thursday, the nineteenth instant, when almost all the town were knotted in the peace of sleep, deaf to all noise and blind to all danger, snoring in calm security and seeing visions of remoteness radiant with the rainbow hues of past associations, or roseate with the gilded hopes of the fanciful future—while the full-faced queen of night shed showers of silver from the starry throne oe'er fields of freshness and fertility, garnishing and suffusing sleepy nature with her balmy brightness, fringing the feathery cottonwoods with lustre, enameling the house tops with coats of pearl, bridging the erst placid Platte with beams of radiance, and bathing the arid sands of Cherry Creek with dewy beauty—a frightening phenomenon sounded in the distance, and a shocking calamity presently charged upon us."

That was just the first sentence! Professor O. J. Goldrick made an enduring mark on Colorado.

Suggested reading: Dee Brown, *Wondrous Times on the Frontier* (Little Rock: August House Publishers, 1991).

EDUCATIONAL HERITAGE IN NEBRASKA

In 1875, when Nancy Higgins was thirteen, her parents moved from their farm near Bethany, Missouri, to Custer County, Nebraska, with eight of their children. Their farm had been an underground railroad station, and continuing resentment from Southern sympathizers led the abolitionist Higgins family to seek free land further west.

The oldest Higgins daughter, with her circuit-riding Methodist preacher husband, had settled in the valley of the Middle Loup River, and the rest of the family homesteaded nearby. Good water was easy to find, but the excellent grazing attracted ranchers, and each group resented the other. Three years later, just ten miles away, two homesteaders—Luther Mitchell and his son-in-law, Whit Ketchum—would have a famous shoot out with the Olive Brothers, ranchers from Texas.

Nancy, the middle child of the nine, became a fine rider and her father's best cattle herder. She herded their stock out to the range land in the morning and back to the fenced stockyard each night. Nancy spent most of her teen years in the saddle, and she could kill a rattlesnake with a whip without getting off her horse.

Nancy had a mind of her own. When she was fourteen, her father brought home a load of supplies, including fabric for new dresses for all six daughters. Unfortunately he got blue for Nancy and she wanted red. She was the only Higgins daughter that fall without a new dress.

The Higgins children attended school in a sod shack, built on their father's land. At nineteen, Nancy went to a Baptist boarding school, about seventy miles from home. A seventeen-year-old brother and a fifteen-year-old sister went with her. They lived together to save money. After one semester, Nancy returned home to teach her nieces, nephews, and neighbor children in a school near her parents' farm.

Nancy had forty-five students ranging in age from four to seventeen. Her first contract, covering two months in spring 1882, paid her twenty-six dollars a month. That fall she moved to the same school she had attended. Her pay stayed the same, but she could live at home, and she only had sixteen students. However, they included two sisters, five nieces and nephews, and a thirteen-year-old brother. Her brother and one nephew gave her trouble. They liked to reach into the sod walls, pinch out clods, and throw them when Nancy wasn't looking.

Also in fall 1882 Nancy met William Gaddis from Iowa who homesteaded three miles away. On October 29, she wrote this poem about William in her attendance book:

I have loved you too fondly
To ever forget
The love you have spoken to me;
And the kiss of affection
Still warm on my lips
When you told me how true you would be,
But I know that I love you
Wherever you roam.
I'll remember your love
In my prayers.

Nancy and William married the next April. William's wedding gift to "Wifey," as he called her, was a custom made pine cupboard. She taught one more term and then helped her husband build their farm up to a fine stock farm of seven hundred twenty acres.

Nancy became a life member of both the Women's Christian Temperance Union and the Women's Foreign Missionary Society. She and William subscribed to the *Chicago Daily News* which came a week or two late. Their children regularly read *Youth's Companion.*

Nancy's brother (not the one who threw the clods) served two terms in the Nebraska Legislature. When the schoolhouse was torn down, the records showed that Nancy was the only woman in the district who had voted in every school election.

William Gaddis had a sixth grade education. He and Nancy had four children. When their sons were seventeen and fifteen, the family moved a hundred miles to Orleans, Nebraska, so the boys could attend a Methodist Seminary. Both graduated from college and became teachers. One received an honorary doctorate. The other taught at the University of Nebraska for eleven years.

Their oldest daughter attended college and taught school.

Nancy and William moved back to the farm when their youngest daughter started high school. She lived with her sister while attending high school. Apparently the youngest daughter did not go to college.

Nancy's mother was her father's second wife. An uneducated hired girl, she was much younger than her husband. When she became a widow, she tried living with various members of her family, but they found it difficult. She always returned to live with Nancy and William.

The educational heritage of Nebraskans was enriched by women like Nancy Higgins Gaddis.

Suggested reading: Mary H. Cordier, *Schoolwomen of the Prairies and Plains* (Albuquerque: University of New Mexico Press: 1992).

PH T DEGREE
(Put Husband Through)

Florence Knisely moved to Kansas in 1878, when she was fifteen. She was born in York County, Pennsylvania, in April, 1863. Her mother often told her that the cannon fire at Gettysburg, two months later, disturbed Florence's sleep, and that she had stood near President Lincoln, her baby in her arms, to hear the famous address.

Florence's father, a Civil War veteran—later a teacher—died when Florence was ten. Her mother had a hard time keeping the family together. They traveled from Pennsylvania with relatives and lived in a tent in the yard of friends in Kansas until they got started farming in Dickinson County on land purchased from the railroad.

That fall Florence would not attend the local school as she already had a better education than the teacher. Instead, she went to Abilene, got a job doing housework at two dollars a week, and started school there. The next April, just before her sixteenth birthday, she began teaching in a rural school for four dollars a week.

The pattern of teaching in rural schools and attending an institute in Abilene for a month or two each fall continued. In 1880, when Florence was boarding six miles from her school, her horse, frightened by wolves, threw her. Her foot caught in a stirrup and she was dragged until unconscious. When she recovered, the wolves were gone. She walked a mile to the nearest house, where she spent the next day in bed. Then she returned to her school, continued riding the horse, and never got thrown off again.

After teaching three years in a town school in Clay Center, Florence started studying summers at Campbell College in Holton. There she met a faculty member, who had come from Indiana the year before to teach. Florence and her professor Charley, tall and scrawny at six feet and a hundred twenty-five pounds, spent an increasing amount of time together as they got better acquainted.

Charley had never met anyone like Florence. The twenty-one year-old girl, dressed more plainly than his other students, had a burning intensity about her that attracted him. She attacked every course with a sense of personal urgency. Her obviously high intelligence pleased him. She carried a heavy course load and carried it so well that he felt he was not doing enough in his own life. The intensity of his response to her personality surprised him.

Not only had she started teaching at fifteen, she was the only child able to earn money and help her widowed mother, with four younger children. Florence's mother and children had moved to Kansas to farm in an unequal but valiant battle with drought, insects, poor land, and low grain prices. And in the middle of all that, Florence was educating herself for better teaching positions and trying to arrange her own life so that she could help educate her younger brothers and sisters!

Charley listened to his new student, awestruck. She showed no self-pity and complained of nothing except her own inadequacies. She was not bitter, but quietly sure that she could do anything she set out to do. She belonged to the River Brethren, a sect that considered ordinary fundamentalist Baptists decadent hell-raisers. And she wasn't smug about that. The things her church was against—card playing, smoking, drinking, dancing, and idleness—were things she had no time for anyway. When Charley took her home to the tiny quarters she shared with her brother Elmer, he knew he was in love. She and Elmer had two attic rooms. The ceilings sloped, and a person could stand erect in the small rooms only in the center.

Florence's friends called Charley her Longfellow. Charley resolved that before he could think of marriage to such a person, he would have to become worthy of her.

Charley's attentions to Florence became a school scandal. It soon became clear that a marriage was not only desirable but wise. That Christmas Charley sent Florence a beautifully illustrated copy of Dante's *Inferno,* which she still had almost sixty years later when she wrote her autobiography.

The next month, in January 1885, Florence and Charley were married in the home of the university president. Florence wore a woolen school dress, trimmed for the occasion with a lace collar. Charley had a new necktie.

Charley squeezed into Florence's tiny room with his trunks and books. Charley made forty dollars a month, but he was paying a back board bill from the year before when he taught without pay. The three of them lived on a dollar a week for the rest of the winter.

Florence and Elmer continued their studies in the university. She earned her tuition by teaching two subjects each term. She taught Geography, Algebra and Mechanical Drawing. Charley and Elmer talked about studying law together after Elmer graduated.

Florence graduated from Campbell University in 1886. Elmer, with whom Florence was always very close, had a year to go. But he died of typhoid fever in December, 1886, a severe blow to both Florence and her husband.

Charley worked so hard in teaching that his doctor advised him to get out of it for his health. He gave up the idea of studying law after Elmer died.

Florence suggested that with her increased teaching income, now that she had the university degree, she could put Charley through medical school.

"But the closest one is in Chicago," Charley said. "That's a long way from Kansas."

"We'll make do."

So in fall, 1887, Charley entered Hahneman Medical College in Chicago while Florence taught in Holton, sending Charley all the money she could spare. They each wrote twice a week, having neither time nor postage money to write oftener.

Charley made good grades, earned preferences, and even won prizes. He sent Florence a sealskin cap for Christmas. When she learned that it cost ten dollars, she couldn't see how he saved that much from what she sent. A sister moved in with Florence, and a brother also came to Holton, but did not move in with his sisters.

Charley came to Holton at the end of the term in February. He found a Dr. Roby in Topeka who allowed him to work free in his office until the next term started. Charley soon decided that he wanted to practice in Topeka when he graduated, so Florence applied at once for the examinations to teach in Topeka schools. She wanted to get a head start there before Charley graduated. She was hired by the Branner school, an elementary school in a low income part of Topeka. As soon as she was settled in, Charley returned to Chicago.

Florence was the only teacher in the school who lived in the school's neighborhood. None of the others wanted to be near "those people." When Florence learned how poorly her students could read, she got permission to use one of the school rooms after hours. Soon she was spending four afternoons a week reading to all who would come. She read almost all of Louisa M. Alcott's works the first winter. Many times the room could not hold all the students who came for the extra hours.

Florence called at the home of every child in her room. Most of the parents were poor, something she understood well. She bought stockings and mittens and mended clothing for mothers tired of sewing and cooking. Sometimes she stayed with the children so their mothers could get out of the house. She got a Presbyterian Church to gather clothing that she made over for the poor children. Florence had never been so busy in her life. If someone had commented on the good she was doing, she would have been puzzled. What else, she would have said, could she do?

Charley graduated in February, 1889, and started working for Dr. Roby for forty dollars a month. Florence continued teaching at the Branner School.

In August, 1890, after eighteen months with Dr. Roby, Charley opened his own office. By then he and Florence were putting her brother

Dave through veterinary school in Chicago.

By Christmas, Charley's practice had grown too much to make calls on foot or with a street car. He bought a horse and buggy, then hired a girl to work in the office.

Florence and Charley bought their first house in 1891. She quit teaching in December, 1892, so they could start a family. Karl was born the following July. A second son, Edwin, came in March, 1896.

Away from teaching, Florence grew anxious about finances. Sometimes she seemed depressed about not having anything to use her incredible energy on. Then, on a trip to Canada in 1897, she got interested in art. She returned home with a reading list of art books to check out of the library. She started writing a newspaper column about art, and then started teaching art to a small group of friends.

Teaching again, she was happy again. Charley saw why teaching had always meant so much to her. He wondered if the world threatened Florence when she wasn't instructing it, supporting it, or in some way managing it.

When Florence was again pregnant, they hoped for a daughter, but their third son, William, was born in October, 1899.

Karl graduated with honors from Harvard Medical School. Two years later he joined his father in practice in Topeka, specializing in psychiatry. When William graduated from Cornell Medical School, he joined his father and brother.

The brothers took formal psychoanalytic training in Chicago. By the end of World War Two, the Menninger clinic and its associates had trained one third of all the psychiatrists in the United States. Karl's book *The Human Mind* was the first book on psychiatry to become a best seller.

A lot of people needing medical help never knew how much they owed to a fine teacher, Florence Knisely Menninger. Charley Menninger made many discoveries about the human mind. But his greatest discovery was not medical; it was his wife.

Suggested reading: Flo Menninger, *Days of My Life* (New York: Richard A. Smith, 1939).

STOUT AS A MAN

Jane Price's reliance on Christian values to alleviate trouble in the world marked her years of teaching, three in Iowa and about twelve in Nebraska. She was also a homemaker, community leader, and farmer, but this pioneer of the prairies never married.

Her mother died in 1858 when Jane was seventeen. Five of her brothers, all under twelve and the youngest only a few months, considered her their new mother. Her father was essentially crippled with rheumatism, but Jane never mentioned that fact in her diaries.

About 1874, Jane, her 61-year-old father, and her two younger brothers moved from Indiana to Iowa, and three years later moved to a farm in Hamilton County, Nebraska. Besides full-time teaching, she managed the farm, although her brothers helped with the labor. She did all the housekeeping and made clothing for nieces and nephews. She bought, sold, and rented more land, and was one of the first women to buy town lots in nearby Phillips. She wrote essays for literary societies, church meetings, and special holidays. She helped organize a temperance society, serving as an officer. When a sister-in-law died, her brother and his family moved in with her, and she took care of those children, as well.

When the Methodists organized a church in Phillips, she and two men each contributed a hundred dollars (about three months' teaching wages) to the building fund. Jane served on the church's Official Board and always sat in the first pew.

When about fifty Indians camped nearby on the Platte River, some of them tried to enter Jane's house. Large and muscular, Jane pushed them out the door.

"Are you a man?" one asked.

"No, but I'm as stout as a man," Jane replied. The Indians went back to their camp and left her alone.

Most of Jane's brothers taught or served as missionaries. Charles, six years younger, served in China. He and his wife were killed in the Boxer Rebellion. Frank, three years younger, also served in China. Fluent in eight languages, he translated portions of the Bible into Chinese.

Jane attended many teaching institutes to improve her teaching skills. She cherished close relations with her students. In February, 1879, when teenager Susie Lutz lay dying, Jane was called to her bedside. She got there just as Suzie died and stayed to wash the body and helped dress it. She wrote that Susie had a sweet smile on her face. "It is better so, as her name was stained in a way that she was in no way to blame for, but must have felt that she is taken from the evil to come."

Jane left no clue about what Susie was not to blame for or why she felt taken from evil.

Two months later, Jane learned upon reaching the schoolhouse that another student, Jennie Tompkins, had died of scarlet fever. She dismissed school and went to the funeral. She described Jennie as "one of the most pleasant and kind-hearted girls I ever knew."

Jane's fortieth birthday entry stated her ideal for life: "I must wait the will of providence and try to follow the guidance of him who holds my destiny in his hand, taking up my life's duties as they come to me and finding my best joy in the service of my heavenly master."

Jane said little about being an old maid. She did write to two soldiers from Indiana in the Civil War. In a letter to one in Tennessee she said she hoped that all the soldiers did not get married before they came home. She was twenty-one at the time.

For two months in fall, 1880, Jane warded off unwelcome attention from a neighbor whose wife died four months before. The last mention of him in her diary was, "I hope I shall have independence enough to let him know that he is not wanted."

Two years later and just after she bought another farm, this one with buildings, she got a proposal from a local preacher she hardly knew. After he offered his "hand, heart, and fortune" she wrote: "I hope he is not much smitten as the case is utterly hopeless."

Jane probably quit teaching about 1890, as her diaries mention teaching less and less in the late 1880s. This independent, committed woman died in 1920. She left town lots in Phillips and Grand Island, 240 acres of farmland, and many grateful hearts in Iowa and Nebraska.

Suggested reading: Mary H. Cordier, *Schoolwomen of the Prairies and Plains* (Albuquerque: University of New Mexico Press, 1992).

SEND MONEY

The following letters demonstrate the similarity usually found in human behavior across modest amounts of time. "Papa" was Stand Watie a noted Cherokee chief who helped arrange for his people to move from their Carolina and Georgia homeland to Indian Territory. He commanded two regiments of Cherokees in the Civil War, fighting for the Confederacy. They fought well at Wilson's Creek in southwest Missouri and at Pea Ridge in northwestern Arkansas. Stand Watie, a brigadier general in the Confederate Army at war's end, surrendered nearly three months after General Lee. Berryville, where daughter Jacqueline wrote from her school, was not far from where her father had fought.

Berryville, Arkansas
April 22, 1871

My Dear Papa

This eaveing is still and I will have no other chance to write to you, and I will give you as good a history of Berryville as I can. Well Cap. Clarke has a very full school . I don't believe I ever went to any better school than he has; for he makes his scholars study now just rite. He dont allow any sweet-hearts to be claimed so I just think he is rite about that. For I dont think its rite for students to have such things as they call sweet-hearts. The students are some of them very far advanced. Oh! I think Cap. Clarke is a splendid teacher. This place dont carry fashons to such an extent; for povity will not let them. But at the examination time we will have big to do. You will come wont you; I would rather you would come than any one else. I will need some money too; for I will have to get some things for the examination, for it will take me from now to get ready. These folks carry fashons to an extence then; for they go well every Sunday. But every day as I told you they go plane and I can keep up with them. Papa you must send me some money, if it is not but $5 for I need it very bad and have been needing it a long time. But if you have $25, send it; for it will take that much to fix me for the exhibition, and more too I expect. And I will need some between now and then. You told me to let you know what it cost; I will send you a sirceler and then you can settle with Clarke. . . .

Well Papa I think this is a very cheap school and good too. I would like to come back here if posable next session; but if it is exposing your povity I will not ask any more, but I think the boading place cant be beat for we are treated just like home folk. We are not treated like strangers. Capt. Clarke has the best mother or as good as ever was, for I like her as if she was kin to me. I am taking mucis lessons and hope to be able to play some for you if you come after me. You must bring Sister with you if you come. The school will be out in July. About the 3rd or 4th. You come about the last day of June and then you will see and here all that is to be heard. But you must be dressed now I tell <u>you</u>. For these people are mity sprucy them times.

Well Papa I expect you are getting tired reading my letter. It is just filled up with nonsense. You may tell Stand William and Tobacco houdy for me. And David too. Well Papa send me some money just as soon as you get it if you have it now send it as soon as you get this. Good bye Papa answer this when you receive it.

Your affectate Child, Jessie.

Like modern teenagers at times in their growth, Jacqueline was dissatisfied with her name and was experimenting with others. She asked her father to address his reply to J. W. Watie.

Papa's reply also will have a ring of remembrance for parents of college children.

Grand River, at The Old Place
May 10, 1871.

My dear daughter:

Your most affectionate and loving letter has reached me. I am happy and delighted to hear from you. You cant imagine how lonely I am here at our old place without any of my dear children. I would be so happy to have you here, but you must go to school. I am glad you are pleased and like the school and your teacher. I am well acquainted with Capt. Clarke. He is a fine man. . . I must try to come to Berryville at the examination. I shall do my utmost to send you back again next term. . . I will try to send the money you require.

Your affectionate father
Watie.

Suggested reading: Dee Brown, *Wondrous Times on the Frontier* (Little Rock: August House Publishers, 1991).

RANCH SCHOOL

Eighteen-year-old Virginia Haldeman had finished her freshman year at the University of Iowa when she went to Wyoming in June, 1903, to teach school. Raised in Iowa, about all she knew of Wyoming came from reading Owen Wister's *Virginian,* a book she hoped to finish before her train reached Denver. Like Mollie Woods, the novel's heroine, she was coming west to teach in a ranch school.

Virginia changed trains in Denver, and her cousins met her at Laramie. They had come out in the 1880s to teach, and one of them had been Albany County Superintendent of Schools.

Virginia had three days to study for her teaching certificate. The examination required two days of continuous writing. She passed and was assigned to a rural school on the Little Laramie River.

The Biddick family, with whom she would board, took her to their ranch, fourteen miles northwest of Laramie. Their three children, nine-year-old Johnny and his older sisters, Edna and Ethel, would be her only students. They had to walk a mile and a half to the school. Virginia hoped it would be a log building, as were all the buildings on the ranch. But it was a white, framed building, just like in Iowa.

Serving as the janitor as well as teacher, Virginia carried in drinking water from the outside pump, brought coal from the shed, hauled ashes out, built the fire, and swept up both after the morning chores and at the end of the school day.

The year before, three children from another family who lived beyond the school also attended, but they had moved away. Virginia doesn't explain why they walked to school when she and her students lived in the same house.

The Biddicks drove a wagon to Laramie every two weeks for mail and shopping. In September a three-day storm brought twenty-six inches of snow, and the rancher had to use a four-horse team on a bobsled with four other men shoveling ahead to break a road into town.

When winter came Edna, who had been taking Latin, moved to the high school department of the University of Wyoming. Then the trustees decided to save expense by having Virginia teach the other two Biddick children in their own home. On Halloween, which was Virginia's birthday, she borrowed a horse and rode twenty-eight miles to visit her sister, who taught at Dutch Flats.

The term ended at Christmas, which Virginia spent with her sister. Then the sister returned to the University of Colorado, and Virginia was assigned another ranch school just four miles from the peak of Laramie

Mountain. That school house, built on skids, had formerly been located at a spring, midway between the Prager and Garrett ranches, which were eight miles apart. In winter, school was held in one ranch house or the other. For this term, the Prager ranch had it for five months. Taxes paid for three months and the Pragers paid privately for two additional months. Virginia got forty-five dollars a month—the same as at the Biddick Ranch—and she paid ten dollars a month board to the Pragers. She saved the rest for college expenses.

Virginia had a room of her own, which she decorated with pennants and photographs until it looked like a typical college freshman room. The Garrett Ranch had mail service three times a week, and the Pragers rode over to the Garrett Ranch to pick up their mail. Virginia heard regularly from her college friends. When the handsome captain of the Iowa football team telegraphed her about an important victory, Virginia's joy knew no bounds. The Pragers lived sixty miles from the railroad. For five months, Virginia never heard a train whistle.

During the day the Pragers set aside a large room in the house for the school. Virginia and her four students, two boys and two girls, sat around a drop-leaf walnut table, similar to the one Virginia remembered from her childhood on a farm. The older Prager girl, Dora, was six months older than Virginia. She studied algebra and Latin. Fred was in the eighth grade, Frankie the seventh, and Sophie the sixth. All were good students.

Virginia kept regular hours. At four o'clock on mail days, the boys saddled their horses for the sixteen mile round trip to the Garrett Ranch. At night the school room became the parents' bedroom.

Virginia enjoyed listening to Mr. Prager tell of his early experiences in the West. Born in Germany, he had freighted with oxen between Omaha and Denver by the time he was twelve. Denver consisted of one cabin on Cherry Creek at that time. A well-to-do bachelor at forty-three, Prager married an eighteen-year-old girl, who also came from Germany. Two years later, they started ranching on Laramie Mountain.

Prager had three thousand sheep. He employed two Mexican sheep herders who lived in sheep wagons but ate in the house. The Pragers brought out supplies from Laramie twice a year. Virginia wondered how Mrs. Prager could always prepare such tempting meals. They had no electricity. They had ninety head of cattle but none were milked. Their milk came in little red cans.

A boy at an adjoining ranch enjoyed visiting the Prager children. He offered to teach Virginia Spanish. Thinking she would have a head start toward additional college credits, she accepted. But when the boy proposed, she stopped learning Spanish!

Every year or so a ranch would host a dance. The Garrett's did it during Virginia's teaching term. The Prager boys drove her over in a wagon. In her ignorance of local custom, Virginia made two big mistakes at the dance.

After several square dances with Fred Prager, she waltzed with a boy who had recently lived in a city. When she realized that they were the only couple left on the floor, Virginia asked to sit out until the music stopped. Later she learned that some did not approve of round dancing for school teachers.

When the music stopped for the midnight supper, Virginia accepted the invitation to eat with the same boy she had round-danced with. Later she learned about that mistake.

Supper at a dance was sometimes the romantic highlight of the evening. Often onlookers buzzed with such questions as these: Had the preferred one asked for a dance before midnight, or did he just file on the supper claim? Did the girl smile and seem happy while dancing with him? Was this their first supper together? Some considered three such shared suppers as equivalent to an engagement. Virginia should have eaten with the Prager boys, who brought her to the dance.

The dance continued all night with a lag in activity around three o'clock and some sitting out. The guests left after breakfast. If you only host a dance every year or so, why not make it last?

Virginia returned to college, married the football captain after he had entered law school, and always had fond memories of teaching at her Wyoming ranch schools.

Eighteen years passed before Virginia visited the area again. Coincidently, her next visit after that came in 1943, the year this writer finished high school in Cheyenne while working for the Union Pacific Railroad. He worked on steam trains which ran through Laramie on their way to Ogden and back.

Suggested Reading: Virginia H. Jones, "Fifty Years Ago," in *Annals of Wyoming*, v. 25 (January, 1953).

SHE DECORATED CLASSROOMS AND MINDS

Sarah Gillespie Huftalen centered her life around teaching. Born in Iowa, she started school near Manchester in 1869 when she was four. Her mother raised turkeys to help pay school expenses for Sarah and older brother Henry. As the children grew they became aware of the abuse their father inflicted on their mother. Once, after he tried to choke Henry, their mother got legal help and forced her husband to leave the family for a year. Sarah was glad at fourteen to move from her country school to the Normal College in Manchester.

When Sarah began teaching in rural schools at eighteen, she had to cope with stove pipes that fell down, spit balls stuck to the ceiling, sixteen-year-old boys who chewed tobacco, and going home with the students as she boarded out with their families. Once she had to rebuff the amorous advances of the married father of one of her students.

Sarah always enlisted the students' help in making the classroom pretty. They washed windows, cleaned walls, hung pictures, and shared the washing of blackboards and the dusting of erasers. As their environment brightened so did their spirits, and their respect for their teacher grew. She hung pictures at their eye level to encourage happy thoughts about scenes of animals, birds, children, patriots, and reformers.

Sarah pioneered in coordinating instruction. The reading class might read about DeSoto, while the geography class drew maps of his travels, and the history class recited about the significance of his discoveries. Geography, for her students, always started at the school house door and traveled over the world. All the grades worked together on projects, and the students developed a strong sense of community.

She thought every farm should have a wood lot. Her students learned about trees, their care and uses, by collecting hundreds of specimens. They memorized poems about trees and made maps of their farms and the school yard, showing the trees and shrubs.

Sarah referred to the trinity of the schoolroom—the child, the teacher, the parents—as the foundation on which all learning was based.

Sarah insisted that each student do his or her very best. She would not accept a paper unless the student endorsed it, "This is my level best." Sarah's students wrote original dialogues and books, which they illustrated and bound. Their work was honored at educational meetings in Iowa and around the nation.

When Sarah was sixteen she met Billie Huftalen, a pawnbroker. At fifty-six, he was older than Sarah's father. Sarah knew she was in love, but said nothing to Billie or her family. Four years later Billie started boarding

SARAH GILLESPIE HUFTALEN

State Historical Society of Iowa

with the Gillespies. Not until he asked her mother if he could marry Sarah, did Sarah reveal how she felt. Henry, just two years older than she, said she should not marry such an old man. Sarah thought her heart would break.

Sarah and Billie suffered in silence until 1892, when they married. Sarah was twenty-seven, Billie sixty-seven. The next eleven years were blissful for Sarah. She continued teaching and became active in temperance work. She had the understanding father-figure she had never known and the loving husband her mother never had.

But Billie went broke in 1903, and Sarah resolved that all of his debts would be paid off. Eight years of saving from Sarah's teaching, and profits from the large garden that Billie tended, paid all the debts.

By then, Sarah was famous nationwide for her educational ideas and methods. She organized the rural teachers—the ones who built their own fires, organized socials to raise money for needed supplies, and taught thirty classes in eight grades—to become a potent force in educational assemblies. She became Page County Superintendent of Schools in 1913. During her term she visited over a hundred schools two or three times each year.

But Billie, now in his eighties, would get lost and confused, and Sarah often had to go home and help her beloved husband. He died in 1914, aged eighty-nine. She wrote in her diary:

"Sometimes I feel his presence, and once he has spoken distinctly. I only wish that we had had a son like him. I cannot understand why childless I had to roam but I expect it is all for the best."

Sarah's despondency over Billie's death ended in 1917 when Iowa State Teachers College made her an associate professor. The next year, while she taught a special class at Upper Iowa University, that school learned that Sarah did not have a college degree. She stayed there teaching, while she completed a four year course in two years and got her own degree. Later she earned her masters degree at Iowa State University.

During her college teaching, Sarah's students ranged in age from seventeen to the seventies. As she had always done, she had them start by cleaning and decorating their classroom. One might wonder how many minds she decorated, directly and indirectly, during the fifty-two years of her teaching career.

Suggested reading: Mary H. Cordier, *Schoolwomen of the Prairies and Plains* (Albuquerque: Univ. of New Mexico Press, 1992).

DEFIANT DAUGHTER

Defiance of her mother led Corabelle Fellows to teach Indians in Dakota Territory. The girl's earliest memories were of her mother telling her and older sister Marian how she wore party dresses as a girl and later studied music, French, and needlework at a ladies seminary in Glens Falls, New York. She wanted her daughters to associate with the best people so they could "marry up to a higher walk in life."

A vivid incident impressed Corabelle when she was about three. They had been living in Glens Falls (apparently near her grandparents) while her father, disappointed that a childhood injury kept him out of the Civil War, was out west looking for gold. He returned and moved his family to Missouri. Corabelle remembered seeing "little pickaninnies" lying on the grass in the hot sun while their mothers worked in the fields. Their crying annoyed Corabelle's mother, who would not "touch the little black things." But she did not object when sympathetic little Corabell dragged the babies into the shade. Her mother said, "Those repulsive little niggers; how can you stand to touch them?" Three-year-old-Corabelle never forgot it.

Corabelle's father was raised in New Hampshire, loved the country, and wanted to be a surveyor. But his wife loved the cities, so he took up photography as a trade. Some time after the incident with the black babies, they moved to St. Louis where he opened a photography shop. After a short period on a rented farm, which Corabelle dearly loved, they moved to Washington, D. C., where her father was a doorkeeper at the Capitol. Her father did not like the city. Her mother had relatives in Congress from both Iowa and Missouri, and she loved living in Washington.

Corabelle and Marian did like the Washington public schools. They had been home schooled in Missouri, and Corabelle considered that six-day schedule too demanding. Corabelle also enjoyed the Library of Congress and the Corcoran Art Gallery.

One day her father announced that he had rented a farm in Virginia. Corabelle was happy again, although her mother dreaded the change. But eventually they returned to Washington, where her father opened another photography studio. Photography produced less income than farming, and they rented the top floor of their four-story house to a 35-year-old British Army officer, with whom 17-year old Corabelle fell in love. When her parents broke up the romance, Corabelle vowed that she would never more follow the social path set out for her by her mother. She judged Washington society women silly to spend their time in endless rounds of parties. She had heard a Senator talk about Indians, and she would go out west and teach them!

Her exasperated parents sent her to an aunt in Illinois where she attended another ladies seminary. She left it early to return to Washington, still resolved to teach Indians.

"Stop talking about your disgusting and loathsome Indians," her mother said. "They'll never be accepted into the best society. How would you go, anyway?"

"The church will send me."

"What church?"

"The Presbyterians."

That set her Episcopalian mother off again. But 20-year-old Corabelle, all of a hundred pounds and one inch over five feet, left for Springfield, Dakota Territory, to teach. Her parting gift was a flat iron. "Try to keep your dresses pressed," her mother said.

Corabelle cried most of the way to Springfield, a small village across the Missouri River from the reservation for the Yankton and Yanktonai Tribes of the Sioux. These were called the Nakota or Middle Sioux. The four eastern tribes, called the Dakota, still lived in Minnesota, the location of all the Sioux when first encountered by Europeans. The seven branches of the Teton Tribe, called Lakota, lived further northwest in South Dakota.

Corabelle arrived in early November, 1884, the coldest day she had ever seen. Two days later she began teaching sewing to a class of fifteen young Indian girls—aged five to eight—on the reservation. She knew no Sioux and her class knew no English. But she "took each docile brown little hand and guided it to set fine hemming stitches in the squares of purple, orange, blue, and scarlet calico which they held." Soon the girls could make their own underclothing.

Alfred Riggs and his wife operated the school. Riggs' father had started teaching Indians in southern Minnesota, and four of his eight children had continued in missionary work.

The girls liked Corabelle and re-named her Wichipitowan, which meant Blue Star. She taught arithmetic to the same small girls and arithmetic and geography to older boys. The girls were more studious. The boys liked to play dominoes. In the evening they would knock on her door courteously and ask for the *can skata* (wood for play).

"How about the lessons?" she would ask.

"Ugh, *Can Skata,*" they said, shaking their heads.

Corabelle would insist that they study a while, before she would hand over the dominoes. She enjoyed watching the boys while they played. They could add up their scores much faster than they could do arithmetic in class. They were never rowdy and never boasted. The winner celebrated with a simple, brief smile, and the next game would begin. She served them hot coffee before they left, and they doted on her. Impressed with her learning, they often repeated with respect, *"Wichipitowan lila ota"* (Blue Star knows many things).

The girls, too, doted on their teacher. She loved to tell them about life in cities and they listened, awestruck and wide-eyed. She had only one dress that resembled their clothing. Gray wool, cut on straight lines, it had a red collar and cuffs, and a long red wrapper ending in tassels. The girls wanted her to wear it all the time. When she wore a skirt and middy blouse, the girls worried. They could not understand why a person five feet, one inch tall would cut her height into two distinct zones.

The boys' quickness in geography surprised Corabelle. They marveled at her descriptions of towns and cities, at the size of the United States, and at its relative smallness compared with the rest of the world. The girls outshone the boys in arithmetic.

The children were all anxious to be noticed. *"He Mye"* (This is I) was their most repeated phrase. Corabelle always tried to recognize their presence and acknowledge their worth.

Corabelle also learned the Sioux language and traditions. After seven months (and the weather was warmer) she transferred to another school at Oahe, north of present Pierre, which Riggs' younger brother, Thomas, operated. Of the seven teachers who had started with Corabelle, only one remained in teaching. The rest could not stand the cold, the food, the Sioux language, and the "magnificent odors" around the Indians. Alfred Riggs told Corabelle that she would find the Oahe school less civilized than his and with a rougher kind of Indian.

At Oahe, Corabelle's only formal teaching was to assist in sewing classes. Her main job was visiting outlying tipis and learning Teton customs. Apparently the Indians were unaccustomed to white visitors, and they were delighted to have her. Once, three small boys sold her a small porcupine for three dollars. She couldn't get the animal to eat, so she asked some women what to do. Each one said, "Oh, give it to me."

Corabelle parted with the animal and then learned that as soon as a quill appeared on the poor little creature, it was harvested. The Teton women valued porcupine quills next to purple calico.

Corabelle did not have the same success with the Teton Lakotas as she had with the Nakotas. The children were supposed to hang their blankets in the cloakroom before entering the schoolroom. The girls, very modest and shy, used the blankets to hide blushing faces and some time passed before they would give the blankets up. The boys never gave in. In open contempt they would carry them into the schoolroom, fold them carefully into cushions, and sit on them.

Corabelle loved to ride and had a saddle sent to her by one of her congressman relatives. Many envied her with her spotted pony and red saddle. She spent many hours on the trail alone. The Indians praised her, saying she had the most prized of Indian qualities, a brave heart.

She also loved archery and learned quickly from one of the boys. When she killed a running rabbit, news of her skill spread over the reservation.

The Indians told Corabelle that their *"Wankan-Tanka"* (Great Spirit) loved best those who showed courage and strength while suffering great pain. In August, 1885, she accompanied a party to witness a Sun Dance in northeastern South Dakota, somewhere near present Sisseton. At that time the dance had been prohibited by the government.

Observing from some distance, she saw the same religious fervor she saw later in a Pentecostal congregation. She saw men push sharpened sticks through flaps of their skin until blood oozed down. The skewers were fastened to a central pole around which they danced. Sometimes a dancer would lean back until the skewer tore free and more blood washed across the dancer's body.

"Stop them! Stop them!" corabelle shouted. "They are killing themselves."

She heard a calm, cool woman's voice beside her. "No, they have strong heart. Mine has a very brave heart."

Later, after the Sun Dance had been completely stopped, Corabelle heard an old Indian ask, "How will the Great Spirit know that the Sioux are still men who can suffer?"

Then she remembered that hot August afternoon and the bloody Sun Dance.

After two years, Corabelle earned a vacation to visit her family in Washington. She wondered again at the uselessness of women at home.

Then she was posted to the Cheyenne River Reservation, a Teton Sioux reservation across the river and a little north of Oahe. There she met Samuel Campbell, the son of a trader and a Sioux mother.

They married in March, 1888, went on a speaking tour, and Corabelle's career in education ended. After they had two sons, her husband left her for an Indian woman. Eventually Corabelle married a Civil War veteran, with whom she had three daughters.

Corabelle's oldest son became a drunk, but she loved him the rest of her life. We don't know how she and her mother felt about each other in later years, but she and her father always remained close.

Suggested reading: Kunigunde Duncan, *Blue Star* (St. Paul: Minnesota Historical Society, 1990).

ROUNDING UP STUDENTS

Twenty-seven-year-old Leoti West left her Iowa home in July, 1878, for Colfax, Washington Territory, where she had agreed with Baptist Missionary S. E. Stearns that she would teach in a school to be started there. She rode trains to San Francisco and steamers to Astoria and up the Oregon (now Columbia) River to Wallula, near the mouth of the Snake River. She thought the scenic grandeur made the Oregon the Rhine of America.

Unable to find accommodations in Wallula, she took the narrow gauge railroad to nearby Walla Walla. She had to ride on rough board seats in a cattle car.

The August afternoon was hot and dusty when she boarded a Concord stage to Colfax. After supper in Dayton, she and the other five passengers reached Pataha City at daybreak for a breakfast of fried chicken on which many feathers "lovingly lingered." Then an all-day trip in a crowded wagon brought her to Colfax. Her two-weeks voyage had cost her two hundred dollars.

Colfax, a village of about a hundred small houses, occupied a narrow gulch between two high, bare hills. On September 11, seventeen students met in the First Baptist Church to begin the first high school in Eastern Washington. But Miss West wanted more students, so she set off on horseback to find them.

Her Indian pony loved treachery when he found the opportunity, but with a rider weighing two hundred pounds he didn't find it often. A short ride brought her to the home of Nelson Davis, Baptist deacon, whose wife had died leaving him with eleven children. Then he had married a widow, Mrs. Stewart, with eleven children of her own, and now they had one together. Miss West said the family of twenty-three children was a Godsend to a struggling school needing students. There was never a year that she did not have one of these Davis-Stewart children in her classes at Colfax. Most of the time she had about eight.

Deacon Davis had a large ranch and was building a new house. When Miss West stopped, blankets and quilts served as temporary partitions. She spent one night and rode on to the ranch of Father Stearns, the pioneer missionary of the region. He lived in a one-room log cabin, about sixteen by twenty. During the week she stayed there, Miss West made excursions into Moscow and Palouse City to recruit students.

One day her hostess—Stearns' sister-housekeeper—took her in a buggy across the mountains to spend the night with a good Baptist family. They lived in a palatial *three-roomed* house with *real* windows. The family promised two students, and fed their guests with potatoes weighing four to five pounds each. Of course, they didn't eat many potatoes. After a night spent fighting bedbugs, Miss West didn't think Baptist bedbugs were any more agreeable than those of other denominations.

Back in the saddle, and this time accompanied by a newly-recruited student, she rode sixty-five miles north to the valley of the Spokane. On the way, they spent the night at the home of James H. "Cashup" Davis, a merchant who got his name from refusing credit. His two daughters, Mary Anne and Charlotte, agreed to become students. Before leaving, Miss West rode to the top of Steptoe Butte and enjoyed the view from the highest point between Spokane and the Blue Mountains of Oregon. The tiny village of Cashup still marks the spot.

After spending a couple of days in Rosalia, where they again fought bedbugs, they rode on to Spokane which had about a thousand residents. They had traveled two hundred miles on their two-week trip at a cost of a dollar and a quarter. Miss West didn't think a Methodist circuit rider could do that well.

"Truly these good people are all friends to the old maid school ma'am," she wrote.

By June, 1879, Miss West had an assistant teacher and over a hundred students. She knew them all by personal experience.

She taught in Colfax for five years, during which time she became a member of the Territorial Board of Education in Olympia. She taught the next eighteen years at the Baker School in Walla Walla, during most of which she was also the principal. When she retired from Walla Walla, she bought a farm in Rosalia and became a teacher there. She also served two years as principal of the school in Republic, Washington, a mining town north of Spokane.

Miss West never married.

At the end of fifty-four years as student, teacher, and principal, someone asked her why her pupils remembered her so kindly and seemed so glad to do beautiful things for her.

"The answer," she replied, "can be given in a single word of four letters."

She didn't have to spell it out. Leoti West was love personified. She also knew how to recruit students.

Suggested reading: Leoti L. West, *A Chapter from the Life of a Pioneer Teacher* (Fairfield: Ye Galleon Press).

REMOTE VALLEY

I n 1896, twenty-nine-year-old Nellie Carnahan arrived in Denver looking for a teaching job. She was born in Wisconsin, the child of two school teachers. Her parents had homesteaded in Dakota Territory when Nellie was seventeen. She attended South Dakota Agricultural College in Brookings and the state normal school in Madison, and then returned to Wisconsin to teach for five years. Then her doctor advised her to go back west for her health.

When she reached Denver, Nellie learned of an opening, but it was late in the fall, and she would have the ride a stage seventy-five miles past the end of the railroad. She spent the winter in Denver.

The next spring a rancher's wife asked her if she would take a one-room school near Lavender, an isolated settlement on Disappointment Creek in Dolores County, Colorado. Although Lavender had only a dozen residents, the Disappointment Creek Valley had fifteen children of school age. Nellie accepted and was told that a member of the school board who was visiting his family in the east would pick her up and bring her to the valley.

Sam Robinson met Nellie in Denver with the news that the bank holding the school district's money had failed. He would have to go on home and find out if the job was still available. If so, he would meet her in Durango, the end of the railroad.

Two cattlemen agreed to guarantee the salary, and Robinson arranged to meet Nellie's train in late November. After Alamoso, only a Mexican woman with a baby, and another woman going to Durango remained in the car with Nellie. The other woman invited Nellie to spend the night with her, but Nellie explained that if she weren't at the hotel when the man came with his wagon, they might think she hadn't come.

"Don't worry," the woman said. "A half hour after we get there, everybody in town will know that the new teacher for Disappointment Valley has arrived. Another teacher in the valley just lasted a week when she came last year. They're looking for a teacher, too."

Robinson picked Nellie up in a light spring wagon for the sixty-plus mile trip to Lavender. As they traveled Nellie learned that Sam had homesteaded seven years before, in 1890, had built a cabin, barn, blacksmith shop, corrals, and irrigation ditches, had fifty acres under cultivation, and had just received the patent to his land the year before. A thirty-one-year-old native of Rhode Island, he had dropped out of Yale as a junior to try his luck in the west.

They stopped to eat the picnic lunch that Sam brought, and reached the valley late in the afternoon. Nellie enjoyed the scenery. Lone Cone, a magnificent mountain almost thirteen thousand feet high at the head of the valley, could be seen for miles.

As they descended a steep slope to reach the road along the creek, their wagon upset, throwing Nellie out. Sam jumped out first and caught her. He laughed as he righted the wagon and recovered her trunk. She didn't see the joke, and chose to walk on down to the road along the creek.

They had not seen a house or a person all day, but now they passed an occasional cabin and saw cowboys riding after cattle. Sam left Nellie at the ranch where she would board. Five of the school's children lived there. Their mother was gone, visiting a sick relative, and the father was out working. Nellie felt tired and lay down for a rest.

"Are you sick?" one of the children asked.

"No, I'm just tired and I thought I'd rest up."

"Well, I never saw anybody go to bed in the daytime who wasn't sick."

Nellie wondered if she had started off on the wrong foot.

Nellie paid fifteen dollars board out of her forty-five dollar monthly salary, and she appreciated the accommodations. She shared a room with the older girls in the family

They rode horses to school, sometimes with as many as three small ones on the same horse. They hung their saddles on the side of the school house and tied the horses to bushes. The log cabin school house shocked Nellie, but she didn't say anything. Fourteen by sixteen, the logs had once been chinked, but most of the mud had fallen out. The children could look out through the walls. The roof, almost flat, was made from mud-covered straw. Dirt often showered down when a wood rat prowled above. Periodically the boys would have to take up the floor boards and recover the pencils, erasers and rulers that the wood rat had deposited there.

Thirteen of her fifteen students were pleasant and bright. The other two were brothers. One could learn but wouldn't; the other would but couldn't. She didn't make much progress with them. Six children came from one family where the mother had died. They did all their own work and always came to school neat and clean. A wholesome, happy bunch, they loved to play pranks on each other, and sometimes on the teacher.

Nellie often rode an old racehorse named Old Coyote. Once, the children lagged behind Nellie on their way home, and then broke into a lope to catch up. Hearing the horses behind, Old Coyote thought he was back at the track. Nellie stayed on, but she couldn't pull hard enough to stop him until they got home. When Sam heard about it, he brought her a different bridle.

"Use this," he said. "It's got a bit that will hold him."

Riding sidesaddle was Nellie's favorite pastime. She spent a month's salary on a new sidesaddle. Twice a week she rode to the post office for the mail.

The family had an organ, and the older girls wanted to learn how to play it. Nellie wasn't a musician, but she knew some of the rudiments of music. She helped them all she could. She often played cards with the adults. They frequently had guests, usually people going through who stopped for the night before riding on to another ranch.

One Sunday, Nellie and the older girls went for a ride and stopped at another ranch where people were shooting at tin-can targets. They wanted Nellie to try. When she put a hole through the tomato on the side of a tomato can, everybody praised her marksmanship. She refused to shoot again, and she never admitted that she was aiming at a can some distance away from the one she hit.

One day she killed a rattlesnake by beating it to death with a stick. She got a good scolding for that from the mother of the family. The snake had twelve rattles and a button.

The social event of the winter was a party at a school house twelve miles away. The children talked of little else at noon recesses for the week before. Nellie's school closed Friday at noon, so they could ride to the other school. Nellie, covered with a Navajo blanket, rode in a hay-filled sleigh. First they went to the homes where they would spend the night. Nellie stayed with the family that boarded the teacher, so they got to visit. The other teacher, tired of the frontier, couldn't wait to get back to Colorado Springs. Nellie thought she was unappreciative, as she had a room to herself with her own washbowl, pitcher, towel, and mirror.

After supper, everyone went to the school house. Seats were arranged around the room, with some pushed together to make a bed for the babies. The young people danced while the men visited in their group and the women in theirs. One woman had never seen a railroad. Her people were pioneers, always moving on before the railroads caught up. Another had never been in a church or heard a sermon. At midnight the women served a lunch and party ended.

Nellie taught a second year. Then she and Sam married and lived on his ranch. Later Sam decided that with two small children and a wife whose health was still frail, they would move to Rhode Island.

Nellie took back pleasant memories of southwestern Colorado and her two years teaching in a frontier school.

Suggested reading: Michael B. Husband (Ed.), "The Recollections of a Schoolteacher in the Disappointment Creek Valley," in *Colorado Magazine, v. 51, p. 141* (1974).

ALASKA TEACHER

When 45-year-old Hannah Breece went to Alaska to teach in 1904 the territory was as much Russian as it was American. The Americans were practically all natives — Aleuts, Kenais, Athabaskans, and Eskimos. The term "Russian" was also applied to the few European residents who were not from that country.

Hannah was an experienced teacher. She had already taught for twenty years in her native Pennsylvania and four years on Indian reservations in the Rocky Mountains. Sheldon Jackson, superintendent of education for Alaska, persuaded Hannah to bring her impressive talents to the far north. She set out determined to bring the blessings of civilization to the nation's less fortunate children and, through education, help them overcome ignorance, poverty, superstition, and disease.

After her excursion steamer reached Valdez, the territorial center for gold and copper mining, she continued west in a smaller vessel, calling at small villages to unload freight, mail, and an occasional passenger. They reached tiny Afognak on an island of the same name, just north of Kodiak Island in a storm. The captain anchored a few miles off the treacherous, rocky coast and lowered Hannah and two crewmen down to the churning sea in a small rowboat. She found shelter in the home of an Aleut woman.

Afognak was actually two villages, two and a half miles apart, one Aleut and the other Russian. She was offered a seat on the best chair or packing box in each Aleut home. Equally welcomed in the Russian homes, she noticed that each of those had a holy corner containing a religious print, an incense lamp, and a bottle of holy water.

Hannah spent her first day in the one-room school supervising the children as they gave it a thorough cleaning. Then the Russian pupils drove all the Aleuts out, saying they were too dirty for the school. Hannah asked the Russian children how many had a grandparent in the Aleut village, and then she proposed a compact: she would be patient and teach the ragged children English if the Russian children would help her tame the wild ones. The Russians agreed, and their ringleader led the Aleuts back into the school.

Hannah wrote to Seattle friends, sending names, descriptions, and clothing sizes for the Aleut children. By the time the "new" outfits arrived, the Russian children were proud of what they had accomplished with their classmates, the parents in both villages were equally proud, and it was no longer possible to tell what village a child came from by appearances.

By November, daily attendance was over a hundred, and Hannah had to divide the school into two sessions, small children in the forenoon and older ones later. Sometimes the young ones stood outside and howled for entrance, but Hannah held to her division. The school and the saloon were the only public places in the villages, and both rooms were well used.

The children learned that an elected president headed their government, and they voted on some decisions in the school, so Hannah thought they understood the concept of a democracy. But one day she asked who chose the president, and the children chorused, "The czar!"

The effort made by the mother of a 14-year-old boy so her son could attend school impressed Hannah. Ephram Derenoff's younger brother already attended the school and Hannah assured his mother that Ephram would be welcome, too. Ephram arrived the next afternoon and never missed a day after that. He already had a head start on the sounds of the English letters, and soon progressed to the Third Reader.

Hannah learned later that Ephram had been living alone on a small, offshore island where he made hay in the summer and tended the family cattle the year round. He fed them when the snow was deep, hunted game for himself, and lived in a small shack.

The father had to harvest wood from the forest for fuel, catch fish in the sea, and shoot an occasional bear to get leather for their boots. The mother could not do any of those things, but she could feed the cows. So she left their Russian home to live all winter by herself in the desolate shack so her son could go to school. Hannah, humbled, wondered how a parent could make a greater sacrifice for a child's education.

Hannah loved the summers on Afognak. The dawn came as early as two in the morning when the dark blue of night gave way to a great burst of gold. Trappers harvested furs all winter, mostly fox, but some marten, mink, and ermine. Hannah bought a Kodiak bearskin and had it tanned into a rug fourteen feet long.

Hannah enjoyed a mild winter, the temperature dropping no lower than ten degrees below zero. But the next winter was bitter. No one could go outside during one three-day storm. Hannah used the bearskin rug as a blanket. Even the sea water froze into a mass of ice along the shore.

At the end of Hannah's second year at Afognak, the community asked her to stay and teach in a new school then being built. But she wanted to move on and got permission to start a school at a remote reindeer station in the interior. She traveled by steamer across Cook Inlet and by a precarious foot trail to Iliamna Village. There she learned that the reindeer station had no children!

The chief of Nondalton, an outlying village, begged her to start a school there. Authorities in Washington, D.C. instructed her to return to the sea, and take a school on Wood Island for a year. She promised the chief that she'd come back if she could.

Across a narrow strait east of Kodiak Island, Wood Island had been a major producer of ice for worldwide distribution, but now it had only a Baptist Orphanage with fifty children. Hannah's one year extended into three as the villagers persuaded her to stay on. Then she returned to Iliamna.

This time she did not have to walk the precarious trail. She had a horse, but no reins or saddle. She almost fell off when the horse, frightened by a bear, bolted and leaped a narrow ravine.

A one-room school and a one-room teacher's home had been built at some distance from the village. The grandeur of the site—a hill that sloped to a river five hundred feet below—reflected the villagers' attitude toward the importance of education.

The village had a Russian church which a priest was supposed to visit every three years, but none had come for five. The one-room home of William Rickteroff, the reader who took the place of the priest, served as the social center of the village. Hannah taught the mothers as well as the children. She had regular classes in household hygiene, sewing, and cooking.

In 1911, at the conclusion of her Iliamna teaching, Hannah spent two months at Nondalton, where she had promised the chief she would return if possible. Nondalton was a remote fishing village which no priest had ever visited, and they had no reader to take the priest's place. Yet the chief had insisted that a church be built. Their religious service consisted of all the inhabitants of the village meeting at the church where they stood for two hours, without speaking. From time to time people would bow or cross themselves, but no one ever spoke or sat down during the "service."

Hannah thought it a pity they did not have in their own language some of the sermons that were then being preached around the world, often to empty pews. The Kenai people in the village assured her that they had never been heathens. Before the Russians came, they worshiped God as the Great Spirit.

Hannah stayed over a second year and then went to Fort Yukon, above the Arctic Circle between Fairbanks and Nome. She went up there just after the Katmai eruption of 1912. Then followed two years at Wrangell and one on Douglas Island across from Juneau, where Hannah fell and broke her leg.

She returned to Pennsylvania where she died at the age of 80. The tidal wave from the 1964 earthquake destroyed Afognak, but the people resettled on Kodiak Island. Their descendants still talk of Hannah Breece.

Suggested reading: Jane Jacobs (Ed.) *A Schoolteacher in Old Alaska* (New York: Random House, 1995).

54

SHE CAME FAR TO A STRANGE LAND

Eight-year-old Johanna Knudsen had had one year of school when her family emigrated from Denmark to Iowa in 1891. She continued her schooling in Iowa, dropping out to teach one year after finishing the 11th grade. She returned to graduate and then alternated rural teaching with study at Iowa State Normal School.

In 1906 Johanna was hired to teach in Bottineau County, North Dakota. She took the train to Bottineau to meet the county superintendent. Impressed with the flatness of the land, the vast space, the large blue dome above the long horizon, she thought the land inspiring and beautiful.

The superintendent assigned Johanna to a rural school four miles from Landa, a tiny settlement forty miles west of Bottineau. She started boarding with the Larsen family, two miles from the school. The teacher, like her students, walked to school.

The term ran from April to December. During the term Johanna boarded with three different families, moving closer to the school as winter approached. She received forty-five dollars a month.

The one-room building had a lean-to for wood and coal, and two privies out back. With the high ceiling, no insulation, and cracks in the walls, tiny Johanna—five feet, one and less than one hundred pounds—struggled to keep the building warm. She used snow to keep the room clean. She would spread it on the floor and then sweep it out with a straw broom.

The stove heated cocoa that made the morning and noon recesses so pleasant. Students often brought potatoes to bake in the ashes. A pot of stew on the top sometimes supplemented the sandwiches they brought in their syrup pails. Some would toast their sandwiches by pressing them against the stove sides.

Johanna had twenty-four students in her school, none in the seventh grade. She emphasized reading, literature, grammar, and spelling. Art was ignored. Science was tied in with the study of animals and plants on the prairie outside the school.

About a third of the students could not speak English. Johanna's Danish allowed her to communicate with the Norwegian children, easing them into the study of English.

All eighth grade students had to take standard state examinations at the end of the year.*

The school had few books, other than regular texts. Johanna brought hers from home to share. When she celebrated her one hundredth birthday at the Westhope Presbyterian Church, she could still remember particular children giving particular declamations.

JOHANNA KNUDSEN

State Historical Society of North Dakota

56

"They always remembered every line," she recalled fondly.

Recesses were exciting with outside games of Pom Pom Pull-away, Hide and Seek, Annie Annie Over, and, when snow was on the ground, Fox and Geese. The teacher ran just as hard as the children; youth was an asset.

After returning to Cedar Falls for another term of normal school in December, Johanna came back in the spring to be assigned to another Bottineau County rural school at Russell. There she taught with Joe Miller, a man who had come to North Dakota to file on a homestead and teach, himself. They married in June, 1908. Paul was born the next April, followed by Margaret (1911), Eugene (1914), and Perry (1916).

Johanna dropped out of teaching from 1909 to 1922. Joe, active in the Nonpartisan League, got involved in politics. He was elected to the state legislature in 1916, and reelected in 1918, 1920, and 1922.

"Joe was not a socialist," Johanna remembered, "but he was always proud that Nonpartisan League legislation produced the State Bank, the State Mill, railroad regulation, and credit for farmers."

Joe died in 1942 and Johanna moved to Westhope to be near her daughter. There she organized bible study groups and boarded teachers, "whom she taught how to teach." With daughter Margaret and three of Margaret's daughters as teachers, Hannah kept up with classroom practice. She enjoyed going over lesson plans, telling stories, and reviewing books.

Granddaughter Bonnie had Johanna visit her classroom in Grand Forks when her grandmother was ninety-five.

"Grandma entered the room and took control," Bonnie wrote. "The children were fascinated as she discussed Danish history and literature and read from Hans Christian Andersen. They said it was the best reading they ever had. She even reached out to the Vietnamese children in the room. She explained to them that she, too, had come from far away to live in a strange land."

*These standard state examinations continued to at least the 1940s. This writer still has the lamp of knowledge pin Bottineau County awarded him when he finished the eighth grade in 1939 with the highest average in the county. The honor really belonged to Lyle Britton, his teacher for five years in a rural school. Britton, like Sarah Gillespie Huftalen, had a master's degree from Iowa State.

Suggested reading: Vito Perrone, *Johanna Knudsen Miller: Pioneer Teacher* (Bismarck: North Dakota Heritage Center, 1986).

57

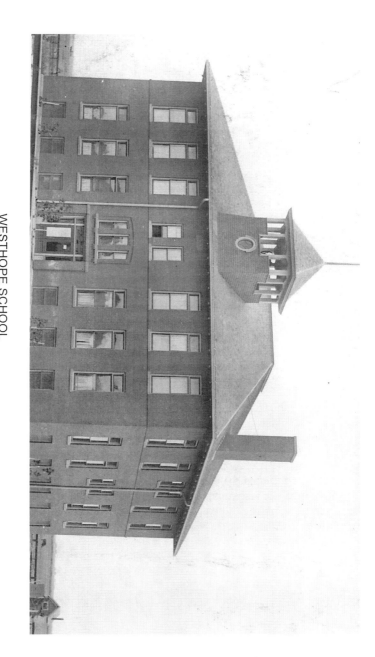

WESTHOPE SCHOOL
Where Johanna Knudsen taught and where this writer attended in his junior year of high school

North Dakota Historical Society

58

A PAIR FOR WESTERN CANADA

In 1892 Elizabeth and John Matheson, married just one year, were posted as teachers to the Anglican mission at Onion Lake in Saskatchewan Territory. This unusual couple and the difficulties they surmounted tell an interesting story of education in early Canada.

Twenty-six-year-old Elizabeth had been raised on a farm, making her own way in the world at fourteen. She taught for three years in the Red River area of Manitoba, during which she met John through family connections. Then followed employment in an orphan's home, a year of medical school, and two years as a missionary in India. She returned from India with malaria, recovered, and married John.

John had been a trader to the Indians, guide, freighter, and railroad construction worker before he married Elizabeth at age forty-four.

Onion Lake was the headquarters settlement for two large Indian reserves, extending two hundred miles north of the North Saskatchewan River. The mission school had both treaty and non-treaty Indians, Métis (half-bloods), and whites. The Department of Indian Affairs provided money only to teach the treaty Indians. John's income from trading and freighting provided for the rest of the family needs.

Before they had been at Onion Lake a year, Elizabeth gave birth to their first child, Gladys. In fall 1894 Elizabeth, pregnant again, had severe mastitis. A Northwest Mounted Police post in Battleford, three days away, had the closest doctor. The stage only went every three weeks.

Elizabeth could barely lift her arm when she arrived, and she trembled with pain. She stayed at the home of a young policeman who had earlier been stationed at Onion Lake. He said there was a banquet that night and there wouldn't be a sober man in town, including either of the two doctors. The next morning one of the doctors, nursing his hangover, came to see Elizabeth. After a cursory examination he went to his instrument bag, returning with a scalpel concealed in his hand.

"You'll feel better now," he said, suddenly thrusting the scalpel into the inflamed breast. Elizabeth passed out from shock. The policeman's wife cried as she dressed the wound after the doctor left. Two weeks passed before Elizabeth was strong enough to go home. This time the Mounties gave her a royal escort, perhaps to make up for their doctor's behavior. Two constables rode in her wagon and two more rode ahead. Carrie Emma was born the next March.

The school enrolment remained at ten to twelve for the first few years, but only six could be registered as treaty Indians and one of those was underage and barred from a grant. John tried to get the department to pay for the non-treaty Indians, mentioning that they were often orphans or deserted by their fathers. The department replied, "It would appear to be a bad policy to put a premium on illegitimacy."

As word of the school's acceptance policy traveled from trapper to trapper, more and more non-treaty Indians brought their children, some from hundreds of miles away. John had known these families as a trader, but it was his skill as a builder that made room for the children. He added an entire wing to the Mission House which could now accommodate thirty more boarding students.

Word of the school's expansion reached Winnipeg, and a volunteer came in 1895. John built more storehouses. He used older boys to help, training them in carpentry skills.

Later in 1895 a tragic incident resulted in Elizabeth resuming her medical studies. An old Cree Indian had frozen his foot, and gangrene had developed. He begged Elizabeth to amputate, but she said she would not dare to do such an operation. With the help of his son, and using only a hunting knife and a saw, the old Indian cut off his own foot.

With the new volunteer now teaching, John suggested that Elizabeth return to medical school. As a doctor, she would be more useful to the mission, since Battleford was three days away.

She left the girls with John's sister at Poplar Point and went on to Winnipeg to live with another of his sisters while she attended a medical college. She soon learned that she was pregnant again. The acting dean, who was her lecturer in obstetrics, attended the birth of her third daughter.

Elizabeth spent the next two years at the Ontario Medical College in Toronto, with summers at the mission. She got her M.D. in April, 1898.

John kept building more rooms and expanding his trade to provide the money. He built a three-story frame school house. By 1905 they had sixty-six children, and Indians came almost daily for medical care.

As the years went on, Elizabeth had six more children, two of whom died in infancy. In 1908 John built a three-story hospital with four wards and an operating room. He died in 1916, aged sixty-eight.

Elizabeth, named principal of the school on John's death, retired in 1941. Seven years later she received an honorary medical degree from the University of Toronto. She died in 1958, aged seventy-two.

This remarkable pair profoundly influenced education and medical care in western Canada.

Suggested reading: Ruth Matheson Buck, *The Doctor Rode Side-Saddle* (Regina: Canadian Plains Research Center, 2003).

WHERE THE FRONTIER LASTED LONGER

We don't know where they came from or what happened to them later, but two Montana school teachers in 1909 and 1910 illustrate how long frontier conditions prevailed in some western states.

Julie Thompson homesteaded near Commanche, a dry, rocky, treeless region in the south central part of the state, in 1909. She built the usual tar paper homestead shack and called it home. When winter set in, time hung heavily on her hands. She learned that ten children of school age lived within twelve miles and had no school to attend.

Julie, enthusiastic, brave, and hard-working, had built a large shack for a homestead — sixteen feet square. She had many years of rich teaching experience before coming to Montana. She offered to teach school in her home.

Julie's oldest prospective pupil — a thirteen-year-old boy — built a crude table and a few benches. Neighbors contributed books. With little of her own furniture to get in the way, Julie's shack soon became a schoolroom.

Some pupils lived so far away they could go home only on weekends. Their parents brought in extra food and stored it in Julie's store room, a cave dug in a bank. Water became a big problem as Julie had no well. A narrow, rutted trail led to the nearest well, two miles away. Once, when a mouse drowned in the water pail the children got quite thirsty before fresh water could be hauled in.

When blizzards came everyone had to stay in the school for days at a time. Then the benches, pushed together, became beds, covered with bedding stored in advance by parents. Feeding the children and caring for them added many chores not usually associated with a one-room school.

One day the wind came up, the temperature plummeted, and by noon a full scale blizzard had swept down on the little school with ten children inside. Snow blew in around the door and window, piling up drifts across the floor. Everyone huddled close to the stove. The water pail, a few feet away, froze over. Julie feared the wind gusts would blow her shack over, the stove would set the wreckage on fire, and they would all perish. The suddenness of the storm caught them with little food inside. The storage cave was impossible to reach.

A little soup, left over from dinner, became supper. The firewood dwindled rapidly, and Julie sent the children to bed early to keep warm. With little wood and no food, Julie despaired about her decision to start the school. What had seemed like a grand adventure to benefit the community had turned into a grim test of survival against overwhelming odds.

Long afterward, an elderly man who had been one of those pupils recalled: "We sang songs and told stories. Miss Thompson kept us as active as possible in that small space. Finally, the wind subsided and the snow became lighter. Suddenly we heard a dog bark and the sound of sleigh runners in the snow. We hurried to the door and there was our neighbor to the rescue, bringing dry wood, food and water."

Julie Thompson received no pay for her teaching. Grateful parents contributed groceries, wood, and water for the school and even fence posts to help her complete her homestead improvements. Julie considered the school an enriching experience and afterward said that the parents' cooperation and the desire of the children for an education made it all worthwhile.

The following spring Ida Southwick came to Savage, a town recently laid out by the Northern Pacific Railroad, about thirty-five miles north of Glendive. Only four women preceded Mrs. Southwick to Savage. We don't know what Ida's husband did, but she had been a teacher.

Most of the three hundred men in Savage worked for the railroad, but itinerants came, looking for work, and homesteaders arrived almost daily. The town had so many children by fall that parents wanted to open a school. No building was available. The first two built were, of course, saloons, but a general store, partially stocked, and a lumberyard were under construction. A crude building had been put up for a temporary church.

The parents held a meeting, elected a school board, worked out a tentative budget, and rented the temporary church. Expenses were prorated among parents according to the number of children attending. Some childless settlers also contributed.

Ida had not intended to teach, but she agreed to take on the school. Thirty pupils had to be taught in one room. They brought a miscellaneous supply of books, and the church offered its folding chairs, but they had no desks. A saloon-keeper volunteered card tables from his establishment. Six pupils sat at each table with books and supplies stored on a shelf eight inches below the table top. Ida learned that the original purpose of the shelf was to hold whiskey, poker chips, and sometimes firearms.

A fine tribute to such teachers as Julie Thompson and Ida Southwick was paid years later by an eminent citizen of early Montana. He said, "Had it not been for [his teacher's] teachings and discipline, I would surely have become a stage robber and renegade."

Suggested reading: Beatrice J. Johnson, "Hazards of the Pioneer School Teacher," in *The West, v. 8, No. 3* (February, 1968).

ORDERING INFORMATION

Our True Tales of the Old West
are projected for 38 volumes.

For Titles in Print,
Ask at your bookstore
or write:

PIONEER PRESS
P. O. Box 216
Carson City, NV 89702-0216
(775) 888-9867
FAX (775) 888-0908

Other titles in progress include:

Californios	Frontier Militiamen
Western Duelists	Ghosts & Mysteries of the Old West
Frontier Lumbermen	Visitors in the Old West
Old West Artists	Scientists & Engineers on the Frontier